PLAYS
BY
LEONID ANDREYEFF

PLAYS

BY

LEONID ANDREYEFF

THE BLACK MASKERS
THE LIFE OF MAN
THE SABINE WOMEN

TRANSLATED FROM THE RUSSIAN BY

CLARENCE L. MEADER AND FRED NEWTON SCOTT

WITH AN INTRODUCTORY ESSAY BY

V. V. BRUSYANIN

AUTHORISED EDITION

NEW YORK
CHARLES SCRIBNER'S SONS
1915

COPYRIGHT, 1915, BY
CHARLES SCRIBNER'S SONS

Published February, 1915

PREFACE

The present versions of "The Life of Man" and "The Black Maskers" are based respectively on the texts printed in the seventh and tenth volumes of the "Collected Works" of Andreyeff, published by the Prosveshchenie Company, of Petrograd; the version of "The Sabine Women" is based on the Russian text published by J. Ladyschnikow, in Berlin.

The spelling *Andreyeff* employed in this volume is adopted to secure conformity with the spelling *Tchekoff* adopted in the companion volume "Plays by Tchekoff." A more scientific transliteration would be *Andreev*.

The translators desire to express their appreciation of the courtesy of the author in extending to them permission to translate the three plays included in this volume, as well as other dramas, and also to acknowledge with gratitude the aid received from Mr. Leonid Borisovich Moiseyeff, of Tomsk, Siberia.

THE TRANSLATORS.

ANN ARBOR, MICH.,
October, 1914.

BIOGRAPHICAL NOTE

THE life of Leonid Nikolaivich Andreyeff has been uneventful. He was born on August 9, 1871, in the city of Orel, which is situated about two hundred miles south of Moscow, in the country of the Great Russians. The father, whose income was always small, died while Andreyeff was a student in the city high school. From that time until his graduation from the law department of Moscow University, at the age of twenty-six, Andreyeff suffered greatly from lack of means, and three times he was led by discouragement to attempt suicide. In childhood and youth he manifested some aptitude for drawing and painting. Indeed, he supported himself in part during his university career in Petrograd and Moscow by painting portraits, but, owing to lack of proper instruction, such endowments as he possessed in this line remained undeveloped. From childhood he was an insatiable reader, and at an early age he had read all the Russian classics and such foreign authors as had been translated into his native tongue. In 1897 he attempted the practice of law, but, meeting with no success and apparently possessing no aptitude for the profession, he turned to newspaper reporting and later to feuilleton writing for the *Moscow Courier*. A number of these early sketches are republished in collected editions of his works. Since 1898 he has devoted himself exclusively to literature, residing first in Moscow and later in Petrograd. In 1906, finding the distractions of a large city too serious an impediment to his literary work, he built a country home on a picturesque site at Terioki, a much-frequented summer resort in Finland. As Terioki is only thirty miles by rail from Petrograd, Andreyeff here enjoys to a large extent the advantages of both country and city. Andreyeff has steadily refused to take an active part in the political life of his day and has never allied himself with any party, believing that party creeds and dogmas are incompatible with the freedom of art.

Very near the beginning of Andreyeff's literary career one of his stories attracted the attention of Gorki, who was at that time at the height of his fame, and who lent Andreyeff much encouragement and assistance. In 1901 Andreyeff suddenly became famous through the publication of a small volume of stories which dealt with certain vital problems of Russian society. Since that time his writings have been exceedingly popular. His plays have been enthusiastically received and have had long runs in the theatres, while the printed editions of his works have been rapidly exhausted. An edition of eighteen thousand copies of "King Hunger," for example, was sold out in a single day. Notwithstanding the intense interest with which his writings have been received, it has been his lot to awaken some resentment and even indignation, and to call forth storms of adverse criticism in some quarters. In this respect his fate has been the fate of Tolstoi and most other great Russian writers, and the opposition to him is accounted for in the same manner. As a critic of society Andreyeff is interested not in the outer events of life, but in character. Consequently his writings are devoted exclusively to the revelation of certain qualities of men's minds and hearts. His pictures of the evils of Russian society are so vivid and the implied censures on society so severe that, although his merits have been fully and cheerfully acknowledged by the reading public as a whole, a certain portion of the public, blinded by passion or prejudice, refuse even to admit the existence of the perverted mental states which Andreyeff, as a great artist and prophet, has seen and described. Such impassioned attacks, however, will be regarded by the sober-minded as an indication of the clearness of his vision, and as a tribute to his marvellous descriptive powers.

THE SYMBOLIC DRAMAS OF ANDREYEFF

"The Life of Man," "The Black Maskers," "The Sabine Women"[1]

Leonid Andreyeff, as a dramatist, is the most interesting product of contemporary Russian literature. Abandoning the older traditions that prevailed from Ostrovski[2] to Tolstoi, and passing by the school of Tchekoff,[3] he brought to the theatre a unique form of art, the rich possibilities of which he is still developing. In 1913 Andreyeff published in the theatrical journal *Maski* a "Letter on the Theatre."[4] This is a "confession of faith," and describes in detail its author's conception not only of the theatre of the past but also of the theatre of the future, to the latter of which he gives the new name "panpsyche."[5] Let us see what this theatre panpsyche is, and how Andreyeff applies his theory to his dramatic productions.

With that spirit of independence which has characterised all great Russian writers, Andreyeff, disregarding long-ac-

[1] Since Mr. Brusyanin, the author of this introductory essay, is a literary critic of note, and at the same time a personal friend of Andreyeff, the essay has the unique value of being an authoritative statement of Andreyeff's own views.

[2] Ostrovski is regarded as the founder of the modern realistic drama in Russia. His literary career extended from 1850 to 1886.

[3] It is interesting to note that the plays of Andreyeff were staged by the same Moscow theatre which introduced Tchekoff to the public.

[4] Republished in 1914 in the *Almenakh Shipovnik* along with another letter on the same subject.

[5] Literally, "all soul," or "all thought."

cepted traditions even now generally regarded as essential, asks point-blank the heretical question: "*Is action, in the accepted sense of movements and visible achievements on the stage, necessary to the theatre?*" In his opinion it is not necessary, inasmuch as modern life itself in its most tragic aspects tends to withdraw farther and farther from external activities and deeper and deeper into the recesses of the soul, into the silence and outward calm that characterises mental life. From this answer to his question one may see how far the theatre panpsyche will depart from the older theatre of Shakespeare, Sardou, Dumas, and other foreign dramatists, and even from the Russian schools that developed out of Ostrovski's art.[1] In this respect Andreyeff is closely akin to Maeterlinck, in whose plays dramatic collisions are not marked by external action, but the problems that characterise the life of the soul, with its premonitions, its yearnings, and searchings, are brought in concrete form before the footlights.

To illustrate his views, Andreyeff draws an interesting contrast between the lives of two men of widely different ages and widely divergent ethical views, Benvenuto Cellini and Friedrich Nietzsche. In reading the memoirs of Cellini, Andreyeff was struck by the large number of events in the life of the mediæval artist and adventurer. "How many escapes, murders, surprises, losses and unexpected discoveries, loves and enmities!" exclaims Andreyeff. "Cellini encounters more events in a short walk from his home to the outskirts of the city than the average modern man does in his entire life. Cellini's life was a counterpart of the life of his day, with its brigands, monks, dukes, swords, and mandolins. In those days interest attached only to a life that

---

[1] All the plays of Ostrovski are marked by conspicuous external action, which is often prejudicial to dramatic truth and inconsistent with the principle of realism.

was full of events, continually active and achieving, whereas a life of inactivity was like a clod lying by the roadside, of which there is nothing notable to be said. Cellini's life is a personification of the older theatre. Read any of the older dramatists, observe any contemporary actor of the older school, and you will realise how much there is of Cellini in them."

In contrast with this, Andreyeff conceives the new theatre as the place for the bodying forth of such intensely dramatic experiences as those of Nietzsche. "Where in Nietzsche's life," asks Andreyeff, "are there events, activities, physical achievements? In his early manhood, while he was a Prussian soldier, and was still to a certain extent a man of action, he was in the least degree a dramatist. The real drama of his life begins just at the time when his life withdraws into the silence and inactivity of the study. It is there that we find the painful re-evaluation of all values, the tragical struggle, the break with Wagner, and the charming Zarathustra!"

The contemporary drama, says Andreyeff, has shown itself powerless to represent the drama of Nietzsche. In the presence of the spiritual and intellectual conflict it is speechless. "Humbly bowing before the immutable law of action, the contemporary drama declines to represent—indeed, cannot represent for us—a Nietzsche, who is so near, so important, so essential to our lives, but continues to offer us in profusion empty, antiquated, and unnecessary Cellinis, with their paraphernalia of tin swords, etc." Andreyeff explains the crisis of the obsolete theatre of to-day by the fact that life itself has withdrawn into the inner recesses of the soul, whereas the theatre has paused at the threshold of these new and profound psychological experiences and intellectual strivings—the struggle of man's thoughts with man—and has never thrown open the door that leads to them.

xiv SYMBOLIC DRAMAS OF ANDREYEFF

In anticipation of the objections of his critics, Andreyeff asserts that he does not in the least mean that events have ceased to occur, that people have ceased to act, or that history has ceased its forward movement. The chronicle of current events is still sufficiently replete with suicides, strife, and war, but all these events in their outward aspects have fallen in dramatic value. Life has become more psychological. In the place of the older passions and the traditional heroes of the drama, love and hunger, there has arisen a new protagonist, the intellect. Not love, nor hunger, nor ambition, but thought in its sufferings, joys, and struggles, is the true hero of the life of to-day. To it therefore is due the first place in the drama. Indeed, Andreyeff has gone so far as to entitle his last drama "Thought"; and if we examine into the plays which he wrote at the beginning of his dramatic career, "The Life of Man," and "The Black Maskers," we shall find in them the same content.

Man, who is the hero of "The Life of Man," and *Lorenzo*, the principal character in "The Black Maskers," are both victims of the tragedy of their intellect, of their obstinate questionings in the realm of thought, and their disenchantments in the sphere of the emotions—the love of life, the love of people, the love of themselves. In "The Life of Man" some fate, embodied in the *Being in Grey*, held in his hands the candle, the emblem of life, and directed the thoughts of *Man* from behind his mysterious veil. Herein lies the whole tragedy of *Man* and *Lorenzo*. From poverty and sorrow *Man* rises to wealth and happiness, and it would appear that with such powerful spiritual weapons as the intellect and the soul he might easily fortify his position. However, the *Being in Grey* turns out to be stronger than *Man*, with his intellect and soul, with his thoughts and his conduct of life. Herein lies the drama of *Man*, whose life has become an "inner" life, while the outward events become non-essential, mere unavoidable details. *Duke Lorenzo* was also strong as far as the external factors of wealth and power were concerned. Yet his restless thoughts, and in particular the one persistently recurring thought that he was not *Duke Lorenzo*, but only the son of his mother and a stable-man, gave rise to an inner, spiritual drama, which overwhelmed the man *Lorenzo* who is hidden behind the duke *Lorenzo*. *Lorenzo* thus slew his double, but he did not come out victorious over the *Being in Grey*. Nothing in his life was changed for the better. In his mind people took on the appearance of maskers, of being other than they really were; all objects in the world were masked and false; even his own thoughts became disguised in masks. The whole world was merely the delusion of *Duke Lorenzo*, who moved about the earth in an eternal mask. Both *Man* and *Lorenzo* are the victims not of outward conditions, but of their own inner experiences.

It is only on the basis of this general theory of the modern theatre that we can understand either "The Life of Man" or "The Black Maskers." But once having accepted this theory we see how baseless are the contentions of Andreyeff's critics. They condemn the external form of such plays as "The Life of Man," which Russian society had universally understood, appreciated, and approved. In framing a play with a new kind of content, Andreyeff instinctively selected new outer forms to correspond. These forms, though intelligible to the public, were incomprehensible to the critics, reared, as they have been for decades, on the dramatic forms of Ostrovski's school.

Consistent with the alterations that have taken place in the drama, Andreyeff calls the old theatre the theatre of "make-believe," as distinguished from the theatre panpsyche, which he calls the theatre of the *truth*. He goes even farther and affirms that the motto of all future art will be "truth in art." When the modern "psychological" novelist or dramatist brings his heroes on the stage, are they the product of the "*play* of his fancy"? asks Andreyeff. "No," he replies, "he experiences them, lives them, creates them, fashions them, any word you choose; only do not use the word 'play.'" For play is something entirely different and distinct from the artistic process of creating new beings, which is the basis of the dramatist-psychologist's art. Play is pretence; and the more refined, cunning, and beautiful, the better it is as play: but psychological creating is truth; and the plainer, the more sincere, the more severe it is, and the farther it is removed from pretence, so much greater will be its artistic value.

"The Life of Man,"[1] when staged, was condemned by the critics on the ground of excessive symbolism and allegory.[2] The author, paying as he did scant heed to the details of daily life that surround the hero of the play and his wife, concentrated all his attention on the conception of *Man* and the life of *Man*. The symbolism employed is very old and familiar—patent, in fact—and is a minor element in the drama. As a matter of fact, this method of picturing human life has long been current among the masses of the Russian people. They picture life either as a candle which blazes up through some mysterious power and finally goes out, or in the form of steps, represented in a crudely drawn picture, in which man is depicted from birth till death. In the first

---

[1] "The Life of Man," published in 1906, was the first symbolic drama written in Russia. Later followed Andreyeff's symbolic dramas, "King Hunger" (the representation of which was forbidden by the censor), "The Black Maskers," "Anatema" (which was taken from the stage on petition of the Moscow clergy), and "The Ocean," which, owing to technical difficulties of inscenation, was never staged.

[2] To appreciate the force of the above criticism the reader must recall that for about a century the Russian public has been accustomed to read only the most realistic form of literature.

half of life—till middle age—he mounts to the summit, then begins to descend the stairs, and finally he reaches old age and his predestined end—death. It is this crude popular conception that Andreyeff takes as the basis of his symbolism; and this selection of a basal motive from the life of the common people is that very truth in art of which Andreyeff speaks, for behind this picture lies the deeply rooted faith of the people in life, and in Fate as the guide of life.

The *Man* whom Andreyeff depicts is an extreme individualist whose whole life is centred upon himself and his own interests, who judges all other persons and all things from the point of view of his own personality. He has made himself the centre of the universe. Nor in this case is fate a mere subjective principle holding sway over man. It is something entirely different. Professor Reisner, in his work entitled "Andreyeff and His Philosophy of Life," says on this point: "Once man has become the foundation of social life, all connecting boundaries and points of contact heretofore existing between him and nature disappear. He is not merely left in isolation, but about him is formed a desert—a vast, social chasm, and the great principle called the law of life now has no means of coming into contact with the naked individual. When this stage has been reached, principles of law and order can find justification only from the point of view of the individual. As soon as the individual has become the unit of society, and the centre of all interests, the aims of this unit must be accepted by it as the aims of the universe, its reason must be accepted as the world reason, and with it the fate of the universe is born and perishes. But if the individual cannot thus establish a direct bond between his personal existence and the law of nature, there results the great tragedy: *Personality renounces the world.*"

Man, the hero of "The Life of Man," failed from the very

first to establish this bond. In his earlier years of poverty he found the meaning of life in the struggle for existence, in dreams of wealth, distinction, and fame. He dreamed even of becoming recognised as a genius. But his dreams all ended in selfish visions of a wonderful villa on the Norwegian coast, where on stormy winter nights he and his wife might find rest and repose in the cheery warmth of the huge fireplace "that burned whole logs." In the ball of Man the hero reaches the summit of life. Observe the feeling of dignified self-importance with which *Man* enters the presence of his guests, his wife leaning upon his arm. He is rich and famous. His guests are filled with admiration for the wealth and luxury of his life, and for his wide-spread fame. But listen! The strains of the polka, hollow and empty, the insipid, soulless dance of the guests and their petty remarks reveal all the tragedy of the petty and empty life of this richest and most famous of men—the profound tragedy that lies in the solitude of *Man* and in the solitude of each and every one of his guests. The egoistic laws of life followed by the *Friends* and the *Enemies* of *Man* hang like a pall over the empty but ominous ball. Like evil forebodings on the eve of death, they reveal all the vanity of human life. In the ball of *Man*, which sums up the entire life of both *Man* and his guests, one does not feel the presence of the great cosmic bond between man and the laws of the universe; but the laws that guide the base *Friends* and *Enemies* of *Man* have brought together here the doomed, and among them the chief of the doomed, *Man* himself, proud, noted, and wealthy; while in the background, seeming to be a part even of the grey wall, is the *Being in Grey* (whether God, Fate, or the Devil, *Man* himself knows not), invisible and frightful in his coldness and indifference, following persistently every step of *Man's* life—the *Being in Grey*, in whose hand is burning—burning out—the candle that symbolises the meaning of the life of this man who has failed to establish a bond between his personal existence and the laws of nature. The beginning and the end of his life are concealed in darkness. "Dragged on irresistibly by time, he will tread inevitably all the steps of human life, upward toward its summit and downward to its end." [1] Still more definitely the *Being in Grey* speaks of the meaning of the life of *Man*: "Limited in vision, he will not see the step to which his unsure foot is already raising him. Limited in knowledge, he will never know what the coming day or hour or moment is bringing to him. And in his blind ignorance, worn by apprehensions, harassed by hopes and fears, he will complete submissively the iron round of destiny."

The "iron round of destiny" is the tragedy of *Man*, conditioned by the strife between the intellect and the emotions, with its attendant sufferings and joys in the case of a man whose strivings toward harmony and order are doomed to clash with the primeval chaos.[2]

The tragedy of *Lorenzo* in "The Black Maskers" is of the same sort. "My soul is an enchanted castle. When the sun shines into the lofty windows, with its golden rays it weaves golden dreams. When the sad moon looks into the misty windows, in its silvery beams are silvery dreams," says *Lorenzo* of his own inner experiences. Yet in the midst of his dreams *Lorenzo* continually asks the question: "Who laughs? Who laughs so gently at the sorrowful life of Lorenzo?" Such were also the dreams of *Man* and his wife, when their distress was soothed for a moment by prayer, and when for a time they had faith in the *Being in Grey*. "*Man*, flattered by his hopes, has fallen into a deep and

[1] See Prologue.
[2] This definition of life is given by Andreyeff in the study published variously under the titles "My Diary" and "Our Prison."

grateful sleep. . . . He dreams that he is riding with his son in a white boat over a beautiful smooth river. . . . He hears the reeds rustle as they part before the boat. He is filled with joy and he fancies that he is blessed. All *Man's* emotions are deceiving him. But suddenly he becomes restless. The terrible truth, penetrating the dense veil of his dreams, has seared his thought: 'Why is your golden hair cut so short, my boy; why is it?' 'My head ached, father, and that is why my hair was cut so short.' And, again deceived, man is happy, and he sees the blue sky and hears the reeds rustling as they part." [1] At the very moment when in sleep his thoughts joyously take wing, misfortune draws close to him; while he sleeps and in his visions finds rest and respite from the iron round of destiny, his son is already dead; so awaking from his dreams he has no course left but to curse the *Being in Grey*. Of this *Being Man* begs not for mercy or for pity, but "only for justice." To this same being *Lorenzo* turns with the prayer: "Who laughs? Who laughs so frightfully at the insane Lorenzo? Have pity on me, O Monarch! My soul is filled with terror! O Monarch, O Lord of the World!—Satan!" *Man* asks no longer for mercy, but only for justice; *Lorenzo* still believes in mercy, and asks for pity. Why the difference? Is not the tragedy of their lives the same? The author himself answers the question by the entire subject-matter of these similar yet different plays. The soul of *Man*, though tortured, still remains intact in the presence of the *Being in Grey*, and he perishes cursing the blind power of Fate; but the soul of *Lorenzo* is rent in twain and his tragedy is the more intense, because Fate, Destiny, God, or the devil is transformed from a vague primordial being into the double of the duke *Lorenzo*. In "The Life of Man" fate appears in the form of an objective

[1] "The Life of Man," Act IV.

principle, a power outside of man; in "The Black Maskers" this same fate has entered, as it were, into the flesh and blood of *Lorenzo*, has become a part of his essence, that is, it has become subjective in the fullest sense of the word. *Lorenzo* considered his life good and beautiful, but having invited his masked guests to his ball he discovered the falseness of his life. In the place of one wife he saw three; in the place of one *Duke Lorenzo* he suddenly encountered at the ball his double. Then appeared also the black maskers, the personification of the darkness of life and the mysterious dark instincts of man. At this point began a new life for *Lorenzo*, and he himself became new, that is, demented. With his doubt as to his parentage—whether he was the son of his father or of a filthy stable-man, his mother's paramour—began the dark, insane life of *Lorenzo*, and he perished in darkness and was burned in his castle, which was set on fire by the jester.

In the midst of the storm of adverse criticism—including such characterisation as "unheard-of horrors," "disregard of real life," "excessive symbolism"—that greeted the first appearance of "The Black Maskers" at the theatre of Komisarzhevskaia, in 1908, very few critics succeeded in making any close approach to a true interpretation of the drama, either in its subject-matter or its form. Yet all were intensely interested, and throngs of "interviewers" made their way to Andreyeff, at his country home in Finland, to learn what he intended in this drama to represent. The author, of course, found it impossible to explain his own creation, but eagerly discussed the symbolic form of this and other plays. "Critics are a strange people," said Andreyeff to one of his interviewers. "They wonder why I write certain things in a peculiar style. The explanation is very simple: every work should be written in the style which it demands. 'King

Hunger' could not be written without symbolism; 'The Seven who were Hanged' could be written only in realistic tones. Tchekoff—the dear, delightful, sensitive Tchekoff, who was always so cautious and considerate in his utterances —finding himself once in a circle of intimate friends and hearing the name of Ibsen mentioned, blurted out: 'Ibsen's a fool!' If Tchekoff did not understand Ibsen's symbolism, could not grasp it, shall I be offended when the critics assail my writings? Eleven years have past since I published my first story. For ten years I have written as I felt. I am not the slave of either symbolism or realism, but they are my servants—now the one, now the other, according to my theme. In the future also I must continue to write as I am able." Not confining himself to the elucidation of the outer forms of his dramas, Andreyeff gives a direct key to the understanding of his "Black Maskers" in "My Diary," published in 1908, two or three months before the writing of "The Black Maskers." The hero of that sketch, an old man who has been immured in a prison since early manhood, writes in his diary: "Every man, as I afterward came to see and understand, was like that rich and distinguished gentleman who arranged a gorgeous masquerade in his castle and illuminated his castle with lights; and thither came from far and wide strange masks, whom he welcomed with courteous greetings, though ever with the vain inquiry: 'Who are you?' And new masks arrived ever stranger and more horrible." To this description the prisoner adds, as a foot-note to his diary: "The castle is the soul; the lord of the castle is man, the master of the soul; the strange, black maskers are the powers whose field of action is the soul of man, and whose mysterious nature he can never fathom." These beings bring into the soul darkness and death, extinguishing the light of life. The "simple" maskers, the guests of *Lorenzo*, are ordinary people; yet even these are transformed and lose their real semblances and, like the black maskers, they become mysterious, incomprehensible, and terrifying to *Lorenzo*, who fails to understand them as he fails to understand his own soul. *Lorenzo's* mind becomes clouded, his own soul becomes repulsive to him, he seems strange to himself. Though he longs to accept his own soul as his own, yet the ugliness, the repulsiveness, of that which he sees within it checks his resolve to do so, and his soul becomes two souls —*Lorenzo* becomes two *Lorenzos*. Before him he sees his double—his horrible, disgusting, false double—and incensed with anger he draws his sword and slays it. Recall the uncanny scene in which the servants, friends, and wife of *Lorenzo* come to bid farewell to the remains of the dead duke, while the duke himself—his other half—stands in the shadow at the head of the bier and observes how they greet the cold corpse of himself. The duality of soul, the duality of personality, has led to the final tragedy of the duke—insanity.

But at this point the author willed that a new transformation of *Lorenzo* should occur. When the castle, fired by *Ecco*, the jester, is in flames, *Lorenzo*, falling upon his knees, calls upon all present to pay homage to the being who is now revealed to his soul, darkened though it be by insanity. "Uncover, gentlemen; it is the Lord God, the Ruler of heaven and earth. On your knees, knights and ladies!" But one conclusion can logically be drawn. *Lorenzo*, passing through this duality of personality and slaying his double, *i. e.*, renouncing the dark and evil elements of his soul, has attained to the knowledge of God and perishes at the moment of attainment.

And the general inference to be drawn from the two plays? Man in Andreyeff's view is in the hands of fate;

whether it appears as the effect upon him of his environment, or manifests itself in the joys, sorrows, temptations, doubts, and struggles of man with his rejoicing, sorrowing, aspiring, doubting, struggling soul. Man is, as it were, condemned to inevitable suffering, and only through suffering can he hope to attain to perfection. Such was the case of *Duke Lorenzo*, whose death brought him a vision of God. In this sense Andreyeff resembles Tolstoi and Dostoevski. The former called upon man to achieve perfection through suffering; the latter admonished man to reject the problems of personality for the sake of perfection. But Andreyeff differs from both Tolstoi and Dostoevski. Recall how the hero of "The Life of Man," despairing of his personal welfare, curses the invisible Being who directs the life of man: "I know not who you are, God, the devil, Fate, or Life, but I curse you! I curse all that you have given me! I curse the day on which I was born! I curse the day on which I shall die! I curse my whole life, my joys and my grief! I curse myself! I curse my eyes, my ears, my tongue! I curse my heart, my head! And I hurl all back into your cruel face, senseless Fate! Be accursed, be accursed forever! Through my curse I rise victorious above you. What more can you do with me? Hurl me upon the ground; yes, hurl me down! I shall only laugh and cry out: 'Be accursed!' . . . Over the head of the woman you have offended, over the body of the boy whom you have killed, I hurl upon you the curse of Man." *Duke Lorenzo*, whose timid soul is rent in twain, calls upon us to worship God; *Man*, whose soul is still intact and unreconciled, curses him who directs both birth and death. Such are the fundamental differences between the two plays.

The third play included in the present volume differs markedly from the other two in its form, its content, and its purpose as conceived by Andreyeff. It transports the author

SYMBOLIC DRAMAS OF ANDREYEFF xxv

from the field of the universal problems of life to the particular conditions of contemporary political life in Russia. It is a satire on the Constitutional-Democratic party. This party is not "legalised" in Russia, and is considered an opposition party both in the Duma and in the country at large. Notwithstanding their repute, however, the "Kadets," as they are called for short, being composed of individuals representing both progressive and conservative elements of society, have a mixed character, which serves to distinguish them from both the socialistic and the populistic parties. Naturally this dual character is clearly reflected in their political activities.

Assuming that in general the subject-matter of the play will be clear to the reader, we will limit ourselves to a few explanations that will enable the reader to appreciate the keenness of Andreyeff's satire. The crude Romans, the abductors of the fair Sabine women, represent the Russian administration of the period of the reaction. The Sabine women are the constitutional "promises" wrung from the government by the revolution of 1905 and 1906. The Sabine husbands represent the Constitutional-Democratic party, who strive by strictly legal methods to preserve these promised constitutional guarantees. The political programme of the Kadets is especially satirised in the second act, at the point when the injured husbands are preparing to march on Rome to liberate their wives. *Ancus Martius* instructs them to march by taking two steps forward and one step backward. The two forward steps are designed to indicate "the unquenchable fire of our stormy souls, the firm will, the irresistible advance. The step backward symbolises the step of reason, the step of experience and the mature mind. . . . In taking it we maintain a close bond with tradition, with our ancestors, with our great past." This is the "progressive-conservative" programme of the Kadets. They failed to gain a victory over their political opponents; or, if they did win a victory, it was just such a victory as that won by the Sabines over the Romans.

In concluding, let us remind the reader that our interpretation of these three plays has been very brief, as has been also our exposition of Andreyeff's views on the theatre. We have set forth but a small fraction of Andreyeff's rich contributions to Russian social thought. Above all, the reader should understand that Andreyeff paints Russian life in true colours, and to know his works is to know contemporary Russia.

V. V. Brusyanin.

Petrograd,
October, 1914.

CONTENTS

	PAGE
BIOGRAPHICAL NOTE	vii
THE SYMBOLIC DRAMAS OF ANDREYEFF, AN ESSAY BY V. V. BRUSYANIN	xi
THE BLACK MASKERS	1
THE LIFE OF MAN	65
THE SABINE WOMEN	157
BIBLIOGRAPHY OF ANDREYEFF	197

THE BLACK MASKERS

CAST OF CHARACTERS

LORENZO, *Duke of Spadaro*
ECCO, *a jester*
DONNA FRANCESCA, *wife of Lorenzo*
SIGNOR CRISTOFORO, *steward of the wine-cellar*
SIGNOR PETRUCCIO, *overseer*
GENTLEMEN and LADIES *of the ducal suite*
MASKERS, *invited by the Duke*
BLACK MASKERS, *uninvited*
ROMUALDO, *a singer*
MUSICIANS
SERVANTS
PEASANTS

THE BLACK MASKERS

ACT I

SCENE I

A luxurious, newly decorated hall in an ancient feudal castle. The walls are adorned with frescoes and hung with paintings blackened with age. Here and there are weapons and statues. The whole room, though brilliant with gold and with bright-coloured mosaics, is delicately tinted by light falling through coloured glass. At the left and in the rear are three semi-Gothic windows half concealed by heavy, gold-embroidered curtains. The rear wall, turning back at a right angle at the centre of the stage, recedes to a row of paired columns which support the upper part of the building. Behind these columns is a spacious, brightly illuminated entrance-hall. Massive double entrance-doors are seen at the right. Directly in front of the spectator, at the point where the rear wall begins to recede, a broad marble staircase with a massive sculptured balustrade ascends to the height of the columns, then, turning to the right, leads to other apartments. The wall above the columns is pierced by several small windows of coloured glass through which comes a peculiar and brilliant light.

The final, hasty preparations are going on for a masquerade ball. The room is flooded with light from many chandeliers and from strikingly beautiful candelabra and sconces. *Several servants in rich but uniform livery hurry from place to place, lighting fresh candles or moving back the heavy armchairs to give room for the dancers. Every now and then certain of them, as if recalling something left undone, rush up-stairs or to the entry doors, the firm, business-like voice of the overseer,* SIGNOR PETRUCCIO, *redoubling their haste and their emulation. Both the overseer and the servants are in high spirits, and the latter, as they come and go, exchange lively jests and quick, fleeting smiles. The gayest of all, however, is young* LORENZO, *the reigning Duke of Spadaro. Well formed, refined of feature, a little languid in manner, but courteous and kindly toward every one, he lightly moves about the hall, all aglow with the joy of anticipation, giving orders, jesting, and urging on the servants, now with cheering words and now with gestures of feigned anger. As he goes he casts happy smiles upon his young wife, the beautiful* DONNA FRANCESCA, *who responds with tender and loving glances. Several ladies and gentlemen, forming the suite of the Duke and Duchess, are also busily engaged, some, like the young Duke, joyfully and eagerly preparing for the reception of the expected guests, others, under cover of the happy confusion, exchanging fond glances, slyly pressing one another's hands, and whispering boldly and quickly into blushing ears. In an upper room somewhere musicians are making ready for the ball, and fragments of musical airs are heard. Suddenly some one begins to sing in a rich baritone, but the song quickly passes over into laughter. Apparently, it is jolly there, too.*

On a rug before a blazing fire the Duke's dog, a huge Saint Bernard, dozes in an attitude of luxurious abandon. Seated near the foot of the stairway, Ecco, *the Duke's* jester, *imitates the Duke's voice and by his orders causes laughable confusion.*

PETRUCCIO. Keep up that speed a little longer, Mario, and you'll be your own grandfather. Hurry, man, hurry!

MARIO. Why, Signor Petruccio, the Duke's best horse doesn't get over the ground as fast as I do.

A SERVANT. When the flies sting.

ANOTHER SERVANT. Or the whip flicks.

PETRUCCIO. Come! lively, there, lively!

LORENZO. This way! More candles here! Don't you see how dark this corner is? No darkness, Signor Petruccio, no darkness!

A GENTLEMAN. [*To a lady*] There! They have driven us out of our last refuge. But I shall kiss you yet.

THE LADY. In the dark it will be hard to find me.

THE GENTLEMAN. In the dark I shall spread my arms wide and embrace the whole night.

ANOTHER GENTLEMAN. You will make a rich haul, Signor Silvio.

ECCO. [*Calling out*] Mario! Carlo! Pietro! Quick! Hold a candle under this gentleman's nose. The darkness frightens him out of his wits.

FRANCESCA. [*To the Duke, affectionately*] My dear! my love! my divinity! How charming your new costume is! You are like a shaft of sunlight flung through the lofty window of our cathedral. Your divine beauty fills me with adoration.

LORENZO. You are a delicate blossom, Francesca. You are a delicate blossom, and the sun, when it kisses you, is overbold. [*He kisses her hand with profound respect and tenderness, but suddenly, in mock terror, calls to the overseer*] But the tower, Petruccio, the tower! If you have forgotten to illuminate the tower I will have you impaled like an unbaptised Turk.

PETRUCCIO. The tower is illuminated, sir.

LORENZO. Illuminated? How dare you say so? It should blaze, it should sparkle, it should rise toward the dark heavens like a huge tongue of fire.

ECCO. Tut! Tut! Lorenzo. Don't show your tongue to heaven or heaven will answer you with a fig.

LORENZO. My dear little fellow, you mustn't annoy me with your jokes. I am looking forward to a feast of light, and your barbed shafts wound me to the soul. No darkness, Ecco, no darkness!

ECCO. Then you must light up your wife's tresses. They are too dark, Lorenzo, too dark. And put a torch in each of her eyes. They are too dark, Lorenzo, too dark.

FRANCESCA. Wretch! Here are so many beautiful ladies —can't one of you win the affections of this miserable jester?

FIRST LADY. He's a hunchback.

SECOND LADY. If he should try to kiss me, his nose would prick me like a sword.

GENTLEMAN. Your heart, madam, would turn the edge of any sword.

> *Enter a gentleman, tall and thin as a pole, the image of Don Quixote. His moustaches droop and seem to be continually wet. He turns gloomily to the Duke.*

CRISTOFORO. I have a shocking piece of news to impart to you, Signor.

LORENZO. What is it? You alarm me, Signor Cristoforo.

CRISTOFORO. I have reason to believe, sir, that we shall run short of both Cyprian and Falernian. These gentlemen [*pointing with his forefinger to the Duke's attendants*] drink wine as camels in the desert drink water.

ONE OF THE SUITE. Signor Cristoforo, why are your moustaches always wet?

CRISTOFORO. [*With dignity*] It is my duty, sir, to test all the wines.

LORENZO. [*Cheerfully*] My good friend, you exaggerate the danger. Our cellars are inexhaustible.

CRISTOFORO. [*Insistently*] They drink wine like camels. Your happy mood pleases me, Signor, but you take things too light-heartedly. When your sainted father and I set out to deliver the Holy Sepulchre——

LORENZO. [*Gently reproaching him*] My dear old friend, you surely are not going to spoil, with your mumbling and grumbling, this delightful evening.

CRISTOFORO. [*Good-naturedly*] Well, well, my boy, don't be angry. [*Threateningly*] Ho, there! Manucci! Filippo! After me! [*Exit.*

LORENZO. But the roadway, Signor Petruccio! Heaven punish you! The roadway! You have forgotten to illuminate the roadway, and our friends will not be able to find us.

PETRUCCIO. The roadway is illuminated, Signor.

LORENZO. Illuminated? Your tongue is like a jaded nag. When the spurs prick its flanks it can only switch its tail. The whole road must sparkle. It must blaze with lights like the road to paradise. Understand me, Sir Overseer. The shades of the cypresses should flee in terror to the mountains where sleep the dragons. Do you lack torches and helpers? Do you lack kegs of pitch?

Ecco. If pitch is lacking, Petruccio, you had better go borrow it in hell. Satan will lend it to you on your personal security.

ONE OF THE SERVANTS. He would have fetched some thence before this but that he feared there would not be enough left to keep him warm.

SECOND SERVANT. Signor Petruccio is so chilly.

PETRUCCIO. Lively, there, lively!

FRANCESCA. [*To the Duke*] You forget me, Lorenzo. Though you light up everything, yet I, unless you smile upon me, am left in darkness. Do the masks interest you so much?

LORENZO. So much, my dear, that I am dying with impatience. There will be flowers and serpents, Francesca. There will be flowers, and serpents among the flowers. There will be a dragon, Francesca. A dragon will come crawling to us, Francesca, and you will see real fire issuing from his jaws. It will be great fun. But don't be afraid. It's all in jest. It's all just our friends, and we shall have a glorious laugh over it. Why don't they come?

A SERVANT. [*Hurrying in*] I was watching from the tower, and I saw something moving along the road, Signor. It looks like a black serpent crawling among the cypresses.

LORENZO. [*Joyfully*] They're coming. They're coming.

ANOTHER SERVANT. [*Running in*] I was watching from the tower, and I saw a dragon crawling toward us. I saw red fire gleaming from its eyes, and I was frightened, Signor.

LORENZO. [*Joyfully*] They're coming. They're coming. Do you hear, Petruccio?

PETRUCCIO. Everything is ready, Signor.

THIRD SERVANT. [*Running in*] There is shouting and commotion at the drawbridge, Signor. They are demanding admittance. I heard the clash of weapons, sir.

LORENZO. [*Angrily*] What! The drawbridge not down? Is that the way to receive my guests, Petruccio? To-morrow I discharge you, if you——

PETRUCCIO. Pardon me, sir. I will run. [*Runs out.*

LORENZO. They have come! Smile, Francesca! They have come!

Ecco. [*Laughs very loudly*] Yes, let's laugh, Lorenzo. We must limber up our jaws. [*Yawns.*

LORENZO. But the musicians! Good. Heavens! Where are the musicians? Has that dunce forgotten all my directions?

FRANCESCA. Don't be angry, my dear. The musicians are in readiness.

LORENZO. But why are they not here?

FRANCESCA. See, now, my love, you compel me to let out the secret. They intended to surprise you. The musicians also are to appear in masks.

LORENZO. And I shall not recognise them? Oh, that is charming! And who planned this surprise? Ah, it was you, it was you, Signora. I can read it in your sly, smiling eyes. But the music! Surely they have not forgotten to learn the piece I composed for them. Oh, this fat rascal of a Petruccio! I shall certainly have to impale him.

Ecco. How indiscreet of you, Lorenzo! Petruccio will steal the stake and run away with it.

LORENZO. Oh! Now I think of it, Ecco, just a word with you before they come. My dear fellow, you may mock me as much as you please; I understand your humour and I like it. But don't, I beg of you, offend my guests. You must not be malicious, Ecco, even in sport. You have a tender heart, my little hunchback, and you are not ill-natured. Why, then, do you sting people with your jests? Laugh. Entertain my guests. Make yourself agreeable to the ladies—and here you may go far—but do not irritate any one. To-day is my day, Ecco.

A SERVANT. [*Flinging open the doors*] They are at the door, Signor.

LORENZO. I'm coming. I'm coming. Call the musicians!

Commotion in the hall. Several MASKERS *appear. The*

costumes are such as are common at masquerades— harlequins, pierrots, Saracens, Turkish men and women, and animals and flowers. But all the faces are concealed under heavy, closely fitting masks. The MASKERS *enter in profound silence and respond to the Duke's courteous greetings with silent bows.*

LORENZO. [*Bowing low and courteously*] I thank you, ladies and gentlemen. I am happy to greet you in my castle. Pardon the carelessness of my overseer in failing to lower the drawbridge and thus causing you some delay. I am greatly mortified, ladies and gentlemen.

A MASKER. [*In a muffled voice*] We arrived just the same. We got in, did we not, gentlemen?

SECOND MASKER. We got in.

THIRD MASKER. We got in.

Strange, muffled laughter from behind the heavy masks.

LORENZO. I am delighted to find you in such good spirits, ladies and gentlemen. From this moment my castle is yours.

A MASKER. Yes, it is ours. It is ours.

The same strange, muffled laughter.

LORENZO. [*Looking about gaily*] But I do not recognise any one. It is amazing, gentlemen, but I do not recognise a single soul. Is this you, Signor Basilio? It seems to me that I recognise your voice.

A VOICE. Signor Basilio is not here.

ANOTHER VOICE. Signor Basilio is not here. Signor Basilio is dead.

LORENZO. [*Laughing*] That's a good joke. Signor Basilio dead? Why, he is as much alive as I am.

A MASKER. Are you, then, alive?

LORENZO. [*Impatiently, but with great courtesy*] Let us leave Death in peace, gentlemen.

ACT I. SC. I **THE BLACK MASKERS** 11

A VOICE. Ask Death to leave you in peace. What need of peace has he?

LORENZO. Who said that? Was it you, Signor Sandro? [*Laughing*] I recognise you, sir, by your melancholy. But cheer up, my gloomy friend. See how many lights there are, how many beautiful, living lights.

A MASKER. Signor Sandro is not here. Signor Sandro is dead.

The same strange, muffled laughter. Other MASKERS *arrive.*

LORENZO. Yes, yes. Now I understand. [*Laughing*] All of us are dead. Signor Basilio is dead; Signor Sandro is dead; I am dead. Excellent! I congratulate you, gentlemen, on your extremely interesting jest. Still, I should like to know who you are— Ah, here come others! Greetings, my dear guests— What a strange costume! Why are you all in red, and what is the meaning of this hideous black snake that is twined about you? I trust it is not alive, Signora. If it were I should pity your poor heart into which it has so ruthlessly struck its fangs.

THE RED MASKER. [*With a muffled laugh*] Do you not recognise me, Lorenzo?

LORENZO. [*Joyously*] Is it you, Signora Emilia? But no, Signora Emilia is not so tall as you, and her voice is fuller and softer.

THE RED MASKER. I am your heart, Lorenzo.

LORENZO. Exquisite! I am sincerely delighted, my friends, that I invited you for this evening. You are so witty. However, you mistake, madam. This is not my heart. There is no serpent in my heart.

ANOTHER MASKER. Is not this your heart, Lorenzo?

LORENZO. [*Starting back, but controlling himself*] You

frighten me, sir, coming so unexpectedly from behind. What? This hairy black spider; this repulsive monster on thin, wavering legs; those dull, greedy, cruel eyes—this my heart? No, Signor, my heart is full of love and welcome. Within my heart all is as radiant as is this castle, which greets you so joyously, my strange guests.

THE SPIDER. Lorenzo, Lorenzo, let us go and catch flies. In a spider-web in the tower yonder something has long been entangled and awaits you. Let us go, Lorenzo. Would you not like some fresh blood?

LORENZO. [*Laughing*] In my castle there is no spider-web. In my tower there is none of that darkness which is necessary to such loathsome creatures as you, my strange guest. But who are you?

THE RED MASKER. Lorenzo, the serpent is restless. It is trying to sting me, Lorenzo. Oh, the pain, the terror of it! Stroke its head, Lorenzo. It has such a beautiful, smooth head, and you see it is not alive. Soothe it, Lorenzo.

Muffled laughter.

LORENZO. [*Falling in with the jest and cautiously stroking the serpent*] When the devil tempts he takes the form of a serpent. But you, of course, are not the devil. You are only a mock serpent, only a mock serpent. [*Hastily*] But, gentlemen, is it not time to dance? The musicians, I presume, have long been waiting impatiently. Petruccio!

A MASKER. [*Approaching him*] What does your Grace command?

LORENZO. Pardon me, sir. I did not call to you. I was summoning my overseer. Petruccio!

THE MASKER. I am Petruccio.

LORENZO. [*Laughing*] Oh, so it is you, you fat old rascal. You, too, have taken a notion to join the sport. And I didn't recognise you. Well, that is very neat. Come, now, tell me— But where are you? Petruccio! Petruccio! Really, I shall have to impale this fat rascal. Hello, there, somebody! Manucci! Pietro!

FIRST MASKER. Did you call me, sir?

SECOND MASKER. Did you call me, sir?

LORENZO. [*Perplexed*] No, I did not call you. [*Grasping the situation and laughing*] Ah, yes, I see. My good fellows, how dare you mingle with the guests?

FIRST MASKER. They told us to.

SECOND MASKER. They told us to.

LORENZO. [*Good-humouredly clapping one of the* MASKERS *on the shoulder*] Quite right. I was only fooling. Let us all be merry on this glorious night— But isn't it odd that I do not recognise any one—positively not a soul—? Why, I've lost my servants again. Mario! Pietro—! Now, really, Signor, isn't that strange? I have lost all my servants.

A MASKER. [*Turning to the others*] Gentlemen, Lorenzo has mislaid his servants.

Loud laughter, the MASKERS *bowing with mock courtesy.*

A VOICE. But where is your suite, Lorenzo?

LORENZO. [*Looking about and smiling*] I see nothing but masks. Here's an interesting situation, gentlemen. Mine being the only real face, I am the only person about whom there can be no mistake.

Renewed laughter.

A VOICE. We are now your suite, Lorenzo.

SECOND VOICE. We are now your suite, Duke. What are your instructions?

Laughter.

LORENZO. [*Very affably, but with dignity*] It is delightful, gentlemen, to find you in such merry vein. I am overjoyed at your charming jest. But I should be deeply offended if you really took my servants' place— Mario!

Other MASKERS *come up. On most of them the tight-fitting masks are replaced by painted faces. The women, however, as before, wear masks of coloured silk. The painted faces of the newcomers are hideous and revolting. Among them are corpses, cripples, and deformed persons. A grey, helpless creature with long legs moves about, frequently coughing and groaning. Seven humpbacked, wrinkled old women run in, in Indian file, capering joyfully and beating castanets.*

LORENZO. [*Bowing courteously*] I have pleasure, my dear guests, in welcoming you to my castle. From this moment it is entirely at your service. Ah, what a charming procession! Tell me, my beauties, where is your bridegroom, the devil?

FIRST OLD WOMAN. [*Running up to* LORENZO] He is at our heels.

SECOND OLD WOMAN. [*Running up to* LORENZO] He is at our heels.

THE TALL GREY CREATURE. [*Bending down to the Duke and coughing*] Why did you call me from my bed, Lorenzo?

LORENZO. [*Lightly*] And where is your bed, Signor?

THE TALL GREY CREATURE. In your heart, Lorenzo.

LORENZO. [*Cheerfully*] How they do slander my poor heart! I am pleased to— [*Staggering back*] What an amazing disguise, Signor! I actually took you for a corpse. Pray tell me the name of the talented artist who so skilfully altered your features.

THE MASKER. Death.

LORENZO. Capital! But if you will permit me to say so, my dear guest, I am sure I recognise in your make-up the beloved features of my friend, Signor Sandro di Grada.

ACT I. SC. I   THE BLACK MASKERS   15

Heavens, but you frightened me, my dear fellow! These masks, these curious masks! Do you know, I can't make out at all who they are. Perhaps you can help me, Signor.

THE MASKER. It is dark, Lorenzo.

LORENZO. But I ordered an abundance of lights. We will have more of them. Petruccio! Petruccio!

THE MASKER. It is cold, Lorenzo.

LORENZO. Cold? Why, to me it seems as hot here as hell itself. However, if you are cold, my dear Sandro, pray come to the fire. Have a goblet of wine. Ho, there, Petruccio! Lazybones!

> *Several* MASKERS, *alike in appearance, run up at the same time and answer almost in one voice.*

THE MASKERS. At your service, Signor.

LORENZO. [*Not understanding*] Petruccio!

THE MASKERS. [*Together*] At your service, Signor. At your service.

LORENZO. [*Laughing*] Ah, I see! A moment ago I lost my servants, and now I have lost my overseer. [*In comic terror*] But here is Signor Sandro come shivering from his grave. Who will give him wine? Pardon me, Signor— Why, he is already gone! Poor fellow! He wants to warm himself. How tired I am! I should like a drop of wine myself. Signor Cristoforo! Has no one seen Signor Cristoforo?

> *A tall, thin* MASKER *approaches.*

THE MASKER. Your orders, sir?

LORENZO. Is that you, my honest friend? I recognise you by your stature. Bring me some wine. This receiving of my guests has wearied me.

THE MASKER. Something is wrong with our wine, Lorenzo. It has turned as red as Satan's blood, and it crazes the brain like the poison of a serpent. Do not drink it, Lorenzo.

LORENZO. [*Laughing*] What could happen to our fine old

wine? You have tasted too much of it and your head is muddled.

THE MASKER. [*Insistently*] I have already seen several drunken guests, Lorenzo. If it is honest wine, why should they be drunk?

LORENZO. Wine, you babbler, wine! [*Drinks the wine, but at the first draught throws away the goblet*] What is this you have given me? It seems as if the fires of hell were licking my throat and burning their way to my very heart. Cristoforo—! Where is he? Pardon me, gentlemen, but really something incomprehensible has happened to our wine— Ah, more maskers! I am glad to greet you in my castle, my dear guests.

> *While* LORENZO, *weariedly bowing ever lower, greets the strange* MASKERS *that are coming in, a subdued hum of conversation fills the hall.*

FIRST MASKER. Whence do you come, Signor?

SECOND MASKER. From the night. And you, Signor, if you please?

FIRST MASKER. I also am from the night.

> *They laugh. Two other* MASKERS *converse.*

FIRST MASKER. He has drunk all my blood. There is not one healthy, living spot left on my body. It is covered with blood and wounds.

SECOND MASKER. He kills those whom he loves.

FIRST MASKER. You know, of course, what is to happen to-day.

> *They move away. Other* MASKERS *converse.*

VARIOUS MASKERS:

— It was idle for Lorenzo to light up his castle so brilliantly. Did you notice as we rode along that something was moving in the shadows of the cypresses?

— I saw nothing but darkness.

— But are you not afraid of darkness?

— Why, I do not think there is anything in it for us to be afraid of. What can the darkness do to us? But are you not sorry for this insane Lorenzo?

— I don't know. Something, I assure you, was moving there.

— See how happy Lorenzo is. Isn't it delightful to have such a cheerful and nimble servant?

> *They laugh. The masked musicians take their places in the balcony.* Ecco *moves about among the legs of the dancers, trying to peer under their masks and arousing laughter by his unsuccessful attempts.*

Ecco. Are you not from the swamps, Signor? It seems to me you are very like the ague which for two months shook me as a dog shakes a rabbit.

> *The* TALL GREY CREATURE *strikes a careless blow and* Ecco *falls.*

Ecco. That's a strange sort of joke! Here am I, the jester, on the verge of tears, while you, at whom I should laugh, are smiling. Oh! who pinched me? Was it you, Signora?

A BEAUTIFUL MASKER. Yes, it was I, Ecco.

Ecco. I observe, Signora, that a hump on the breast deforms a character no less than a hump on the back.

> *The* BEAUTIFUL MASKER *swiftly and silently strikes the jester a blow with her dagger. The glittering edge glides across his neck and the jester runs whimpering up the staircase and thence clambers out onto one of the marble projections. Laughter.*
>
> *The musicians begin a wild melody in which are heard malicious laughter, cries of agony and despair, and some one's low, sad plaining. The dance of the* MASKERS *is also strange and wild.*

LORENZO. I am glad that you are merry, my friends. Though for my part I am a little weary— But what sort of music is this? Heavens! how wild it is and how it pierces one's ears. Luigi, are you drunk or crazy? What are you playing there with your band of disguised brigands. Pardon me, my dear guests, this donkey Petruccio has spoiled everything.

A MASKER IN THE ORCHESTRA. We are playing what you gave us, sir.

LORENZO. [*Nettled*] You lie, Luigi. Lorenzo could not compose such a hellish discord. I hear in it the wails of martyrs under merciless torture. I hear in it the laughter of Satan.

THE OLD WOMEN. [*Running up with castanets*] The bridegroom is coming. The bridegroom is coming. The bridegroom is coming.

LORENZO. Pardon me, my charming jesters, but I must first admonish this bold-faced rascal, Luigi.

A MASKER IN THE ORCHESTRA. Luigi is not here, Signor.

LORENZO. Then who is speaking? Is that you, Stampa?

THE MASKER. No, it is another. We are playing only what you gave us, Signor.

LORENZO. [*Laughing*] Ah, I see. The tones are masked. Capital! Do you hear, ladies and gentlemen? To-day the very tones are masked. Really, I was not aware that tones could put on such repulsive masks. Isn't it droll?

A VOICE. And you had never learned that, Lorenzo? How little you know.

ANOTHER VOICE. It's certainly your own music, Duke.

A THIRD VOICE. But where are you yourself, Lorenzo?

Laughter. The music continues. The old women with the castanets run forward.

THE OLD WOMEN. The bridegroom is coming. The bridegroom. The bridgroom is coming.

LORENZO. [*Bowing low*] I crave your pardon, my dear sir, for not greeting you as I should, but there are so many persons here and I recognise no one of them—positively not one. Just conceive of it—I do not even recognise my own music. It's extremely amusing, isn't it?

A MASKER. But do you recognise yourself, Lorenzo?

LORENZO. Myself? [*Laughing*] To be sure. You see that I wear no mask— But what is this?

> *A strange procession moves slowly past the Duke. A young, proud, and beautiful queen is led in by a half-drunken groom, who embraces her. Before them walks a peasant nurse carrying in her arms a misshapen infant, half animal, half man.*

LORENZO [*In great agitation*] What is the meaning of this, Signors? Even under the disguise of masks such a union seems to me unseemly and repulsive. And what is this that is borne before them? What a disgusting mask!

A MASKER. The groom had intercourse with the queen and this is their charming son. Make way for the queen's son!

THE GROOM. [*Drunkenly*] Hey there! Knights! Crusaders! Out of the way! Drive them off, my queen, or they will harm our precious son.

Laughter.

VOICES. Way for the queen's son!

LORENZO. [*Turning away much agitated*] I am not at all pleased with this jest, Signors— Hello, Ecco, you rascally jester, why have you climbed up there? Why are you not entertaining the company with your pleasantries?

ECCO. [*Weeping*] I am afraid of your guests, Lorenzo. They have hurt me. Send them away, Lorenzo.

LORENZO. [*With rising anger*] Who has dared to affront you? It cannot be. My honoured guests are too kind and courteous to injure any one. It is more likely that you, you rascal, having given offence by your malicious wit, are now shielding yourself from punishment.

ECCO. [*Weeping*] Your guests are fine people, Lorenzo. My hump is swimming in blood. It is like a hilly island in the sea. Haven't you a little costume for me, Lorenzo? I, too, wish to put on a mask.

LORENZO. Come here.

The jester, glancing about timorously, comes down to LORENZO.

ECCO. What do you wish? Speak quickly or I will run away. I am all in a tremble.

LORENZO. I also am somewhat fearful, my dear Ecco. I don't quite understand what is going on. Who are these persons? I don't recognise one of them, and I think there are more than I invited. It's strange. Can't you recognise anybody, Ecco? Their faces, to be sure, are covered, but you are so good at recalling their bearing, voice, and figure. You, perhaps, have recognised some one.

ECCO. Not a soul. Let me go, Lorenzo.

LORENZO. [*Sadly*] Do you, then, desert me, my dear Ecco?

ECCO. I am going to put on a mask.

LORENZO. Very well, my little hunchback. Go, if you are frightened. But send Donna Francesca to me. Do you know where she is?

ECCO. She is up-stairs. Send them away, Lorenzo. I will run to summon her. [*He goes up-stairs.*

LORENZO. [*Addressing a newly arrived and very beautiful* MASKER] Greetings, Signora. You are as entrancing as a vision. You are as delicate as a silvery moonbeam, and I reverently bend my knee before you. [*He sinks on one knee and respectfully kisses her hand, then rises*] I see only the graceful outline of your figure and your little foot, but permit me, my divinity, to be so bold as to look into your eyes. How they shine! Even through the meshes of this black and hateful mask I see how beautiful they are. Who are you, Signora? I do not know you.

THE MASKER. I am your falsehoods, Lorenzo.

LORENZO. [*Laughing*] Can a lie, then, be as beautiful as you are, Signora? But you mistake. There are no lies in me. I hate a lie, my lady. If you knew Lorenzo's thoughts, his clear, pure thoughts—if you knew his soul, which sings in the heavens as the lark sings in spring above the flooding Arno— [*Frightened*] Ah, what's this?

> *Something formless and shapeless, with many arms and legs, creeps up. It speaks with many voices.*

THE THING. We are your thoughts, Lorenzo.

LORENZO. A bold jest! Still, you are my guests. I invited you——

THE THING. We are your overlords, Lorenzo. This castle is ours.

LORENZO. [*Clasping his head*] Oh, this horrible music! It is enough to drive one mad. Luigi, or somebody there—I do not recognise any one—I beg of you, I command you—play what I gave you. Unmask the tones. Don't you remember how beautiful the melody was that I composed? A little sad it was, gentlemen, I confess. In truth, I often yield myself to a tender and languorous melancholy. But it was so full of harmony, so pure, so pellucid. If, perchance, you have forgotten it, Luigi, listen—I will recall it to you. [*He begins singing a lovely melody. After the first two measures, however, he takes up the air that the musicians are playing and breaks off in alarm*] How absurd! You put me out, gentlemen. My head is somewhat dizzy. Really, something was wrong with the wine. How absurd, gentlemen! My brain seems to have turned to melted lead.

Loud laughter.

A VOICE. Why did you break off, Lorenzo?

SECOND VOICE. Lorenzo is drunk. Lorenzo, Duke of Spadaro, is drunk.

Laughter.

SECOND VOICE. We were ready to hear you, Lorenzo; we know what a great artist you are.

THIRD VOICE. Sing, Lorenzo; we insist.

LORENZO. [*With dignity*] My friends— [*Frightened*] Ah, who are you? Who touches me on the shoulder? Madam, the guests are all assembled, and you are an intruder. I do not know you.

A BEAUTIFUL MASKER. It is I, my love.

LORENZO. Pardon me, madam, but only my wife, Donna Francesca, may address me thus.

THE MASKER. [*Laughing softly*] Do you not know me, Lorenzo?

LORENZO. Something about you, my charming masker, reminds me of my wife. But this black mask— Permit me to look into your eyes. Out of a million women I should know my beloved by her eyes. [*He gazes into her eyes, then laughs joyfully*] Francesca, my love, how you frightened me! Why are you masked? You know— [*He leads her to one side and, pressing her tightly to him, speaks almost in a whisper*] My dear, I am so weary, and my heart pains me as if a serpent were stinging it. My thoughts are in confusion. You have seen that frightful monster—look! Over yonder! It's in the corner now. It says it is my thoughts. But, Francesca, my dear, my beloved, that is not true, is it?

THE MASKER. It is only a mask, Lorenzo.

LORENZO. [*Doubtfully*] Do you really think so, Signora? And will they go, and shall we be left alone?

THE MASKER. Yes, we shall be left alone. [*Passionately*] And I shall hold you so tightly, Lorenzo, that you will think I have never embraced you before.

LORENZO. [*Absently*] Yes? I am very happy, my lady— But these masks—this horrible Signor Sandro is painted so like a corpse as to deceive any grave-digger. It seemed to me that I saw worms. I would not put on so frightful, so revolting a mask even in jest.

THE MASKER. [*Frightened*] Signor Sandro? Why, Signor Sandro is really dead. My dear, you have made a mistake.

LORENZO. [*Slowly*] Why do you mock at me, Francesca? If he were dead I should have had notice of his death.

THE MASKER. And so you did, Lorenzo. You have forgotten, and you are weary. Your hands are cold. I must kiss your hand, my love, even though they are watching us.

She kisses his hand. Another beautiful MASKER *approaches from behind and speaks in a loud voice.*

THE SECOND MASKER. Lorenzo, did you send for me?

LORENZO. [*Horrified*] Francesca's voice!

THE SECOND MASKER. Ecco said that you wished to see me.

LORENZO. Ecco? [*Slowly pushing away the* MASKER *whom he had embraced and looking at her in horror*] But who are you, Signora? And how dared you deceive me? I have done you honour—I have embraced you. [*He pushes her away gently*] Leave me.

THE FIRST MASKER. [*Wringing her hands*] Lorenzo! Lorenzo! Would you drive me away? What ails you, Lorenzo?

THE SECOND MASKER. [*Impatiently*] Did you send for me, Lorenzo? Who is this lady who presumes to speak to you so affectionately?

LORENZO. Francesca! Francesca! [*In perplexity he looks now at one and now at the other.* *Approaching the* SECOND MASKER *and knitting his brows in an expression of horrified inquiry, he gazes into her eyes*] Your eyes, your eyes—show me your eyes. Yes, it is you, Francesca. It is your soft and tender gaze. It is your beautiful soul. Give me your hand. [*To the* FIRST MASKER, *with contempt*] And you, madam, leave me.

THE SECOND MASKER. [*Pressing close to the Duke*] Lorenzo, your maskers frighten me. Our castle is overrun with monsters. I saw Signor Sandro. He is horrible.

LORENZO. [*Clasping his head*] Signor Sandro? Why, he is dead. You told me so yourself.

A third equally beautiful MASKER *approaches from behind and speaks in a loud voice.*

THE THIRD MASKER. Lorenzo, my dear, did you send for me? Ecco said that you wished to see me. Who is this lady with you? And what is the meaning of this unseemly familiarity, Lorenzo?

LORENZO. [*Stepping back with a laugh in which is heard a note of insanity*] What a capital joke, madam, what a delicious farce! Now it is my wife who is lost. Laugh, my dear guests. I had a wife. They called her Donna Francesca, and I have lost her. What a strange jest!

THE THREE MASKERS. [*Together*] Lorenzo, my beloved!

LORENZO. [*Laughing*] Do you hear, gentlemen?

General unrestrained laughter.

VOICES. Lorenzo has lost his wife. Weep, gentlemen. Lorenzo has lost his wife. Give Lorenzo another wife.

On all sides are heard plaintive female voices: "Here I am, Lorenzo. Here I am, Lorenzo. Take your Francesca." *From somewhere comes a single terrified voice:* "Save me, Lorenzo, I am here." *Loud* laughter. *The seven old women, with the air of coy and embarrassed brides, seem about to throw themselves on* LORENZO'S *neck.*

VOICE. We will give Lorenzo a wife. Gentlemen, Duke Lorenzo is now contracting a new marriage. The wedding march, musicians!

The MUSICIANS *play wild strains remotely resembling wedding music, but the music is that which is played in hell at the masquerade wedding of Satan. The* RED MASKER *with the serpent approaches* LORENZO.

THE RED MASKER. Do you recognise your heart now, Lorenzo? [*Plaintively*] Caress the poor serpent, caress the poor serpent. It has drunk all my blood.

THE SPIDER. Now do you recognise your heart, Lorenzo? Let us go up into the tower, my friend. Something is entangled in the spider-web there and waits for you. But is your sword sharp, Lorenzo? Is your sword sharp?

LORENZO. Hence, hence! Brood of darkness, I know you not. [*Running a few steps up the staircase, and raised thus alone above the throng of* MASKERS, *he tries to cry out, but suddenly presses his hand to his heart, and, smiling sadly, comes down again, the same winning, candid, noble, and handsome figure as before*] Pardon me, my dear friends, for my touch of ill-humour. These choice jests, these adroit tricks of yours have just a little dashed my spirits— And I have lost my wife— Her name was Donna Francesca. Permit me now— since the hour of departure draws nigh—permit me to call your attention to some real music—not the hideous discords with which this disguised brigand of a Luigi has, in his desire to contribute to the general gaiety, so tortured our ears, but some music of my own. I am a very poor composer, gentlemen. It is rare that these earthly ears of mine are ravished by celestial melodies. But you will not criticise me too harshly. In the virgin purity of the tones you will find a restful calmness and the reflection of some one's heavenly vision— And I have lost my wife, gentlemen, I have lost my wife. Her name was Donna Francesca.

THE MASKERS. We are waiting for your music, Lorenzo. All the world knows the enchanting music of Duke Lorenzo. But the hour of departure is still remote.

LORENZO. I am at your service, my dear guests.

[*He confers with the* MUSICIANS.
A little before this the first of the BLACK MASKERS *has appeared in the hall—a strange, deformed creature like a living fragment of darkness. Glancing about timidly and suspiciously, wondering at everything new, strange, and unfamiliar, the* BLACK MASKER *steals guiltily along the wall and awkwardly conceals itself behind the other* MASKERS. *Every one whom it approaches starts back perplexed and alarmed.*

A VOICE. Who is this? This is not a masker.

SECOND VOICE. I don't know. Who invited you, sir?

The BLACK MASKER *makes no answer, but, shrinking into itself, quietly hides behind the others. Two* MASKERS *converse.*

FIRST MASKER. [*To the other in a low voice*] How many of us were there?

SECOND MASKER. A hundred.

FIRST MASKER. But now there are more. Who is this? Don't you know?

SECOND MASKER. Not I. But I am afraid to speak of it. It seems that they fly toward the light.

FIRST MASKER. Crazy Lorenzo! He lighted up his castle too brilliantly.

SECOND MASKER. Lights are dangerous in the night.

FIRST MASKER. To those who are abroad?

SECOND MASKER. No, to him who lights them.

LORENZO. My friends, I beg your attention. You see this masked gentleman. His name is Romualdo and he is an admirable singer. He will now render for you a little ballad which I made bold to compose. Have you your notes, Romualdo?

THE MASKED SINGER. I have, sir.

LORENZO. And the words? Consult your notes frequently. In one place, my friend, you often go wrong.

THE MASKED SINGER. I have the words also, sir.

LORENZO. Luigi, you villain, if you make a mistake in a single note I will have you hanged from the castle wall to-morrow.

A MASKER IN THE ORCHESTRA. You will have no occasion to waste rope on me, sir.

LORENZO. Attention, ladies and gentlemen, attention. [*Much excited*] Now, Romualdo, do your best, my friend. Do not disgrace me, and to-morrow I will give you a costly belt.

> *The accompaniment begins with a beautiful, soft, and tender harmony, pure and clear as a cloudless sky or as the eyes of a child; but with each successive measure which the masked artist sings the music becomes more fragmentary and more restless and soon passes over into wild cries and laughter, expressive of tragical but incoherent emotion. It closes with a solemn and melancholy hymn.*

THE MASKED SINGER. [*Singing*] "My soul is an enchanted castle. When the sun shines into the lofty windows, with its golden rays it weaves golden dreams. When the sad moon looks into the misty windows, in its silvery beams are silvery dreams. Who laughs? Who laughs so tenderly at the mournful dirge?"

LORENZO. Right, right, Romualdo.

THE MASKED SINGER. [*Singing*] "And I lighted up my castle with lights. What has happened to my soul? The black shadows fled to the hills and returned yet blacker. Who sobs? Who groans so heavily in the black shadows of the cypresses? Who came at my call?"

LORENZO. [*In perplexity*] That is not there, Romualdo. What kind of music is that?

THE MASKED SINGER. [*Singing*] "And terror entered my shining castle. What has happened to my soul? The lights go out at the breath of the darkness. Who laughs? Who laughs so horribly at insane Lorenzo? Have pity on me, O Monarch. My soul is filled with terror. O Monarch—O Lord of the World—O Satan!"

THE MASKERS. [*Laughing*] Have pity on him, Satan.

LORENZO. That is false, singer. I, Lorenzo, Duke of Spadaro, Knight of the Holy Ghost, could never have called Satan the monarch of the world. Give me the notes. My sword shall teach you how to read. [*Snatches the notes and reads with growing horror*] "And my soul is filled with terror, O Lord of the World—O Satan." That is false. Some one has imitated my handwriting, gentlemen. I never wrote this. I swear by almighty heaven, sirs, I swear by the sacred memory of my mother, I swear by my word of honour as a knight. There is some base deceit here. The words have been altered, gentlemen.

THE MASKERS. We have no need of your oaths, Lorenzo. Go to the church if you want to repent. We are the masters here. Continue, singer.

LORENZO. [*Smiling feebly*] Pardon me, gentlemen, I had for the moment forgotten that for me everything is changed—faces, tones, even words. But who would have thought, my dear guests, that words could assume such revolting masks. Go on with your jest, singer.

ACT I. SC. I **THE BLACK MASKERS** 29

THE MASKED SINGER. [*Singing*] "In the black depths of my heart I shall erect a throne to you, O Satan. In the black depths of my thought I shall erect a throne to you, O Satan. Divine, immortal, almighty, from now on and for ever hold sway over the soul of Lorenzo, happy, insane Lorenzo."

Applause. Laughter.

VOICES:

— Bravo, Lorenzo! Bravo, bravo!
— Lorenzo is the vassal of Satan.
— We kneel to you, Lorenzo.
— Lorenzo, Duke of Spadaro, is a vassal of Satan.
— Bravo! Bravo!

LORENZO. [*Crying out*] In God's name, gentlemen, we are all deceived. This is not my singer. This is not Romualdo but some impostor. Satan has sent him here. Something frightful has happened, gentlemen.

A VOICE. He sang your own song, Lorenzo.

SECOND VOICE. Out of your own mouth he confessed to Satan.

LORENZO. [*Pressing his hand to his heart*] This is a horrible falsehood, gentlemen. Just imagine, my dear guests—how could I, Duke Lorenzo, Knight of the Holy Ghost, son of a crusader——

A VOICE. But did your mother tell you whose son you are, Duke Lorenzo?

> *Laughter.* LORENZO, *extending his arms, tries to say something, but his words are inaudible. Pressing his hands to his head, he runs swiftly up the staircase. Cries:* "Way for the queen's son!" *Two* BLACK MASKERS *appear, one after the other.*

A VOICE. Who is this? Our numbers increase.

A FRIGHTENED VOICE. Uninvited guests are coming. Uninvited guests are coming.

THIRD VOICE. They fly to the light. Off with your mask, sir. [*He tries to pull the black mask from the face of the stranger and springs back in terror, crying*] They are not masked, gentlemen.

General confusion. Everything is enveloped in darkness. The wild music, however, continues, gradually receding.

Curtain.

SCENE II

From somewhere in the distance come sounds of music, which, mingling with the howling and whistling of the wind that rages about the castle, fill the air with a wild, tremulous melody.

An ancient library in the castle tower. A low, massive oak door, partly open, through which steps are seen leading down and a little beyond other steps leading upward. The heavy ceiling is vaulted and there are small windows in deep stone recesses. Here and there on the walls and hanging from the ceiling are spider-webs. Everywhere are large old books —on the floor, in heavy, iron-bound chests, and on small wooden stands. A portion of the wall, hollowed out in niches, is also used to hold books. Some of the niches are draped with heavy curtains.

Beside one of the open chests, which is full of papers yellowed with age, LORENZO *is seated on a low stool. Near him, on a support, stands a wrought-iron lantern which, by reason of its cross-bars, throws here dark shadows and there bright lines of light. For some time there is profound silence. All that can be heard is the far-off music and the rustling of the sheets of paper as* LORENZO *turns them over.* LORENZO *is dressed as at the ball.*

LORENZO. [*Raising his head*] What a frightful wind there is to-day! For three nights now it has been raging and grows steadily more violent. How horribly like the music of my thoughts! These poor thoughts of mine! How like frightened creatures they beat about within this tight box of bone! Once Lorenzo was young, but now, though only a little time has passed—though the sun has encircled the earth but twice —lo, he is old, and the weight of terrible experience, the horrible truth of things human and divine, has bowed his youthful back. Poor Lorenzo! Poor Lorenzo! [*He reads. Breaking off for a moment*] If all that is in these yellowed papers is true, who then is ruler of the world, God or Satan? And who am I that call myself Lorenzo, Duke of Spadaro? Oh, the horrible reality of human life! My young soul is smitten with sorrow. [*He reads, then carefully lays aside the sheets and speaks*] So it is true, mother; it is true. I thought, my mother, that you were a saint. I swore by your memory, and my oath was as solemn as if I had sworn upon my knightly sword; and yet you, my saintly mother, were the paramour of a drunken, thieving groom. And my noble father, returning from Palestine to die in his ancestral home, learned of this and pardoned you, and bore the terrible secret with him to his grave. Whose son am I, O my saintly mother— the son of a knight, who gave his life's blood to the Lord, or the son of a filthy groom, an abominable traitor and thief, who robbed his master at his orisons? Poor Lorenzo! Poor Lorenzo!

> *He falls into deep thought. Swift footsteps are heard along the staircase, and* LORENZO *rushes into the room, his head between his hands, in the same attitude in which he left the hall. He takes his hands from his face, sees the* LORENZO *who is seated, and cries out in a frightened voice.*

THE SECOND LORENZO. Who is this?

THE FIRST LORENZO. [*Rising in alarm*] Who is this?

> *The* SECOND LORENZO *throws himself upon the other and hurls the lantern to the floor. The room is now faintly illuminated by the light from the open door. There is a brief, muffled struggle and then the two figures separate.*

THE SECOND LORENZO. Your jest is overbold, sir. Remove your mask, I command you, else I will remove it for you by force. I gave you my castle but not myself, and by assuming my mask you insult me. There is but one Lorenzo, but one Duke of Spadaro, and that is I. Off with your mask, sir! [*He advances toward the other.*

THE FIRST LORENZO. [*In a trembling voice*] If you are only a frightful apparition, I conjure you, in the name of God, vanish. There is but one Lorenzo, but one Duke of Spadaro, and that is I.

THE SECOND LORENZO. [*Wildly*] Off with your mask, sir! I have borne too long with your unseemly jests. My patience is at an end. Either remove your mask or draw your sword. Duke Lorenzo knows how to punish insolence.

THE FIRST LORENZO. In God's name!

THE SECOND LORENZO. In the devil's name, you mean, unhappy man. Your sword, sir, your sword, else I shall run you through on the spot like a guilty dog.

THE FIRST LORENZO. In God's name!

THE SECOND LORENZO. [*Furiously*] Your sword, sir, your sword!

> *From the dimly lighted stage comes the whistling and the clash of meeting rapiers. The two* LORENZOS *engage each other savagely, though the* FIRST LORENZO *is obviously the inferior. There are brief, muffled exclamations:*

"In God's name!"
"Off with your mask!"
"You have killed me, Lorenzo."

He falls and dies. LORENZO *sets his foot upon the corpse and, wiping his sword, speaks with unexpected sadness and tenderness.*

LORENZO. I am sorry for you, Sir Impostor. Your strength of wrist, your deep breathing, showed me that you were young like myself. But your misfortune, unhappy sir, lay in this, that Duke Lorenzo wearied of laughing at the amiable quips of his guests. You went to an obscure death, young man, the hapless victim of a masquerading joke; but still I pity you, and if I knew where your mother is I would bear to her your parting words. Farewell, Signor.

He goes out. For some time there is silence. Then all is veiled in darkness, and the sounds of wild music grow louder and draw nearer.

Curtain.

SCENE III

The ball continues. There seem to be more MASKERS. *The hall is more crowded, and the* MASKERS *are restless as if the strange, mysteriously altered wine were having its effect upon the guests. The music, though it has grown a little languorous, is as wild as before. A mournful and lovely melody springs up, as it were accidentally, in the chaos of wild and turbulent cries, but is immediately overwhelmed and swept away upon the wind like a withered leaf which, torn from its branch, flutters in circles before it sinks to rest. Part of the* MASKERS *continue to dance, but the greater number, perplexed and restless, move to and fro, gathering for a moment in groups to interchange brief, excited remarks. The* BLACK MASKERS *wander about singly in the throng. Hairy and black from foot to crown, some resembling orangoutangs and others those uncouth hairy insects which in the night-time fly toward the light, they move along the walls with a guilty, embarrassed, and somewhat absent air and hide in the corners. But curiosity overcomes their shyness, and, creeping cautiously about, they examine various objects, holding them close to their eyes. They touch the white marble columns with their hairy black fingers. They take in their hands the costly goblets, only to drop them again, as it were, helplessly. The* MASKERS *who arrived before them are manifestly afraid of them.*

VOICES: Where is Lorenzo?

— Where is Lorenzo? We must find Lorenzo. Did no one notice where the Duke went? We must tell him now or it will be too late.

— They fly toward the light.

— It is plain that they are here for the first time. See how they look at everything, with what curiosity they touch things. Who invited them?

— They were not invited. They came of their own accord along the lighted road.

— But perhaps they are some of our friends.

— No, no, they are strangers.

— It is all due to the light in the tower. How dreadful!

— Crazy Lorenzo! Crazy Lorenzo! Crazy Lorenzo!

— The drawbridge should be raised. Then they cannot enter.

— Call Lorenzo.

A BLACK MASKER *touches, out of curiosity, the sleeve of one of the other* MASKERS, *who springs back affrighted.*

THE MASKER. What do you wish, sir? I do not know you. Who are you? Who invited you here?

THE BLACK MASKER. I do not know who I am. Some one lighted up the tower, and we came. It's dark out there and very cold. But who are you? I do not know you, either.

> *He tries to embrace the* MASKER, *but the latter shrinks from him.*

THE MASKER. Keep your hands from me, sir, or I will hew off your fingers.

> *The* BLACK MASKER *moves unsteadily toward the fire burning on the hearth and sits cross-legged to warm himself. His fellows join him and in a black ring encircle the fire, which immediately begins to die out.*

FIRST BLACK MASKER. It's cold, it's cold.

SECOND BLACK MASKER. It's cold.

THIRD BLACK MASKER. Is this what they call fire? How beautiful it is! Whose house is this? Why didn't we come here before?

FIRST BLACK MASKER. Because we were then unborn. The light begat us.

SECOND BLACK MASKER. Why does the fire go out? I love it so, and yet it goes out. Why does the fire go out?

A MASKER. Duke Lorenzo is a traitor. He has played us false. He said the castle was ours. Why, then, did he invite these creatures?

SECOND MASKER. He did not invite them. They came of themselves. But this castle is ours, and we will have the drawbridge raised. Ho! Servants! Servants of the Duke Lorenzo! This way!

> *No one comes.*

THIRD MASKER. The servants have run away. Call Lorenzo. Call Lorenzo.

THE OLD WOMEN. [*Running up with castanets*] The bridegroom is coming. The bridegroom is coming. The bridegroom is coming.

VOICES. Lorenzo! Lorenzo! Lorenzo!

LORENZO *appears, smiling, on the staircase. His clothes are torn. On his bared breast is a large blood-red spot, but he seems not to be aware of it and bears himself with his former dignity and with the refinement and reserve of a prince regent.*

LORENZO. Kindly pardon me, my friends, for presuming to leave you for a moment. You can't imagine, my dear guests, what an amusing and diverting trick has been played upon me. I have just met a very clever gentleman who had donned the mask of Duke Lorenzo. You would have been amazed at the striking resemblance. This skilful artist had stolen not only my dress but even my voice and my features. Really, it's amusing. [*He laughs.*

A MASKER. There is blood on you, Lorenzo.

LORENZO. [*Glancing at himself indifferently*] It is not my blood. I think [*rubbing his forehead thoughtfully*], I think I killed that jester. Did you not hear falling bodies, gentlemen?

A MASKER. Duke Lorenzo is a murderer! Whom did you kill, Lorenzo?

LORENZO. Pardon me, gentlemen, but really I do not know whom I did kill. He lies in the tower, and if you like you may take a look at him. He is lying there. But why has the music ceased? And why, my dear guests, are you not dancing?

A MASKER. The music has not ceased, Lorenzo.

LORENZO. Oh, really? I thought it was the wind, merely a violent wind. Dance, my friends. Your unbounded joy delights me. Petruccio! Cristoforo! More wine for my dear guests. [*Sadly*] Ah, to be sure [*he laughs*], I have lost them all—Petruccio, Cristoforo, and Donna Francesca. So my wife was called—Donna Francesca. A charming name, isn't it? Donna Francesca——

The number of the BLACK MASKERS *increases. One of them mounts the stairs and addresses himself to the Duke.*

THE BLACK MASKER. Did you kindle the light?

LORENZO. Who are you, sir? You have a strange, coarse voice, and I think I did not invite you. How did you gain admittance?

THE BLACK MASKER. Did you kindle the light?

LORENZO. Yes, my charming stranger. I had my castle lighted up. The lights shine far, do they not?

THE BLACK MASKER. You roused the whole night. Everything is astir there, and now the night is coming hither. No harm in our coming, was there? Is your name Lorenzo? Is this your house? Is this your light?

He seeks to embrace LORENZO, *who violently thrusts him away.*

THE MASKERS. [*From below*] Be on your guard, Lorenzo. Lorenzo, your castle is in danger. They have come uninvited. Have the drawbridge raised and all the doors tightly barred.

A VOICE. The drawbridge is already raised, but they are clambering over the walls.

ANOTHER VOICE. All the darkness of the night is transformed into living creatures, and from every side they are coming hither. Bar the doors.

A MASKER. [*From below*] Lorenzo, you invited us, and we are your guests. You must protect us. Summon your armed guards and kill these creatures. Otherwise they will kill both you and us.

A THIRD VOICE. Look! For every one of them a light

goes out. They devour the light. They put the light out with their black bodies.

FIRST VOICE. Who are they? They love the light and yet they put it out. They fly to the light and the light goes out. Who are they?

LORENZO. What a delightful jest, Signors! It's very clever of you. But the lights are actually going out, and it is becoming strangely cold here. May I trouble some of you to call my servants? They will bring fresh lights. I really do not know where they are.

> *The closed doors burst open, as if suddenly yielding to a strong pressure, and let in a throng of* BLACK MASK-ERS, *and at the same instant the light grows markedly fainter. The* BLACK MASKERS, *roaming about the hall with the same embarrassed but persistent curiosity, gather in a black throng around the fireplace, completely extinguishing the already enfeebled blaze.*

THE BLACK MASKERS. It's cold, cold, cold.

VOICES. Relight the candles. They are going out. Who opened the doors? Bring torches. Torches!

> *In the confusion that ensues several of the guests try to close the doors, but give back before the pressure of the continually increasing throng of* BLACK MASKERS. *Others, with no greater success, attempt to light the extinguished chandeliers, which flare up but immediately go out again. Now and then a* MASKER *appears with a blazing torch, the red, flickering light filling the hall with a fantastic dance of shadows.*

LORENZO. [*Watching the scene with pleasure*] A charming sight. A more interesting conflict between light and darkness it has never been my good fortune to witness. A thousand thanks to him who devised it. I am his devoted, lifelong servant.

VOICES. The torches are going out. Bring torches.

A MASKER. We must put out the lights in the tower. This insane Lorenzo will ruin us all.

SECOND MASKER. Some one has already gone to the tower.

THE SPIDER. [*Speaking to a* BLACK MASKER *toward whom he has for some time been making his way*] Are you from Satan?

THE BLACK MASKER. Who is Satan?

THE SPIDER. [*Incredulously*] Why, don't you know Satan? Who sent you here?

THE BLACK MASKER. I don't know. We came of our own accord.

He tries to embrace THE SPIDER. *The latter, frightened, runs away on wobbling legs.*

LORENZO. Luigi, you villain, why are you and your orchestra silent? Play, I beg of you, that song of mine— Do you remember it? Pardon my weak voice, gentlemen; I must refresh the memory of this forgetful singer. Listen, Luigi.

He runs over the opening bars of a simple, touching air, such as mothers sing when they lull their children, and strangely, with low and tender harmonies, the strains of the orchestra answer to the song. All else is silent.

THE BLACK MASKERS, *in awkward and ungainly attitudes, listen to the music, gaping with vacant curiosity. Only at the door, which the* MASKERS *hold shut by the main strength of their shoulders, there is a knocking and scratching and a low, plaintive moaning.* LO-RENZO, *closing his eyes and swaying slightly, sings in a low voice. Suddenly, behind him, along the stairway, echoes the trampling of many feet, distinctly audible in the silence. Several* MASKERS *run down the staircase past* LORENZO, *jostling him.*

LORENZO. [*Gently reproaching them*] Gentlemen, you put me out.

ONE OF THE MASKERS. [*Panting*] Murder! Murder! There has been a murder in the tower.

VOICES. Who is murdered?

FIRST MASKER. Lorenzo himself—Lorenzo, the Duke of Spadaro, lord of this castle—is murdered.

SECOND MASKER. We saw his corpse. The unhappy Duke lies in the library, pierced by a rapier thrust from behind. His slayer is not only a murderer but a traitor.

LORENZO. That is false, gentlemen. I struck him in the heart. I slew him in honourable combat. He defended himself savagely, but the Lord God strengthened my hand, and I slew him.

VOICES. Vengeance, gentlemen! To arms, to arms! The Duke of Spadaro is treacherously slain.

FIRST MASKER. [*Pointing to* LORENZO] And there is his murderer. Off with your mask, sir!

LORENZO. My mask? [*With dignity*] It is true, gentlemen, that I killed some one in the tower—some brazen jester—but it was not the Duke Lorenzo. I am Duke Lorenzo.

VOICES. [*Shouting*] Off with your mask, murderer!

> *Meanwhile the influx of the* BLACK MASKERS *and the quenching of the lights continue. Now and then another torch replaces one that has gone out. The ensuing words of* LORENZO *and the* MASKERS *are interrupted by frequent cries of* "Bring torches, the lights are going out."

LORENZO. Why do you think that I am masked, gentlemen? [*Feeling of his face*] This is no mask. I assure you, gentlemen, this is my own face.

VOICES. Off with your mask, murderer!

LORENZO. [*Flaring up*] I beg you to give over this unbecoming jest. I swear on my honour that this is the face that God gave me when I was born, and not one of those repulsive masks that I see on you, gentlemen. A mask cannot smile as I smile in answer to your daring jests.

He tries to smile, but his lips only twitch convulsively. For a moment, with teeth bared, he presents the appearance of a frightful, laughing mask, but instantly his face becomes motionless, turns pale, and stiffens.

LORENZO. [*Horrified*] What is this? What has happened to my face? It does not obey me. It will not smile, but grows rigid. [*Piteously*] Perhaps I am going insane. Just look at me, gentlemen. This is surely not a mask. It is a face—a living, human face.

Laughter and shouts: "Off with your mask, murderer! Look, look! Lorenzo is turning to stone."

LORENZO. [*His face turned to stone*] All is lost, gentlemen. I tried to smile and could not. I tried to weep and could not weep. I wear a mask of stone. [*He grasps his face in a fury, trying to tear it off*] I'll tear you off, accursed mask, I'll tear you off together with the flesh and blood. Help me, Donna Francesca. Cut the edge here a bit with your dagger and it will at once fall away and let you see the face of your Lorenzo. Bring your consecrated sword, Cristoforo. Save your master, whom God has abandoned. One moment, gentlemen, one moment—I will——

He utters a wild cry and falls. At the same instant there is a crash of breaking window-frames, the windows are burst open, and through them pour in the BLACK MASKERS. *The hall is dark save for the tremulous light of two remaining torches, and presently one of these goes out. A commotion arises on the darkened stage. There are wild cries of terror and despair and vain efforts to escape. Several of the* BLACK MASKERS *mount the musicians' balcony, seize the horns, and trumpet wildly.*

A Voice. Do you hear? They are blowing the trumpets. They are summoning their kin.

Second Voice. That is their music.

Third Voice. Save yourselves, they are coming through the windows!

First Voice. The tower is full of them. They are pouring down from it like a black torrent. Bring torches.

Fourth Voice. There are no more torches. This is the last.

Many Voices. Save yourselves, save yourselves!

Third Voice. They hold all the exits.

A Female Voice. He is embracing me. I am stifling. I shall die. Save me! Among so many knights is there none to protect me?

A Voice. To arms!

Third Voice. Swords are powerless against them.

Fourth Voice. There is no way of escape. We are lost! Crazy Lorenzo! He has ruined us all!

The Black Maskers. [*Roaming about, one by one*] It's cold, cold. Where's the light? Where's the fire? They have deceived us!

A Voice. [*In rage and despair*] You have devoured the light, you brood of darkness!

The Black Maskers. It's cold, cold. Where is the light? Where is the fire?

> *They crowd around the last torch, which one of the Maskers holds high in his uplifted hand, seeking to keep it alight. The torch goes out. Darkness.*

Voices. Crazy Lorenzo! Crazy Lorenzo! Crazy Lorenzo!

Curtain.

ACT II

SCENE IV

A corner of the chapel in the feudal castle.
The walls are draped in black in sign of mourning. The tall, dust-laden windows of coloured glass admit a feeble, softly tinted light. On a black dais, in a massive black coffin, lies the body of LORENZO, *Duke of Spadaro. At each corner of the coffin is a huge wax candle. On the dais at the head of the coffin, in the soft glow of the candles, stands* DUKE LO-RENZO, *dressed entirely in black, his hand resting on the bier.*
From the courtyard of the castle comes at intervals the whining and barking of hunting-dogs. Now and then a prolonged and mournful blare of trumpets carries abroad the sad news of the death of the Duke of Spadaro. In the intervals of silence the solemn notes of an organ and the voice of a priest can be heard at one side beyond the glass doors leading to the other half of the chapel. Mass is being conducted there uninterruptedly.

LORENZO. [*To the one lying in the coffin*] The whole neighbourhood has by now been informed of your death, Duke Lorenzo, and in tears is calling for vengeance on your murderer. Lie still, Signor. Those who loved you are now coming to pay their respects to your dust. The peasants will come, and your servants, and your inconsolable widow, Donna Francesca. But I beseech you, Lorenzo, lie quiet. I have already had the honour of running my sword through your unworthy heart, but if you stir, if you dare to speak or cry out, I will tear your heart clean from your breast and throw it to your hunting-dogs. In the name of our former friendship, I beseech you, Lorenzo, lie quiet. [*He arranges the shroud with tender solicitude and kisses the corpse on the forehead. At this moment in the corner of the chapel, in the folds of the black drapery, is heard a deep sigh and the plaintive tinkling of bells*] Who's there? Oh, is that you, my little Ecco, hidden in the corner and softly tinkling your little bells? Who let you in?

Ecco. Why did you die, Lorenzo? Foolish Lorenzo! Why did you die?

Lorenzo. I had to die, Ecco.

Ecco. Then I shall die with you, Lorenzo. Your servants use me ill. Your dogs' teeth are sharp. All day I lay hid in the tower, waiting for the door of the chapel to open. Do not drive me away, Lorenzo.

Lorenzo. You shall stay here, jester.

Ecco. What a long, white nose you have, Lorenzo. It must be embarrassing to have such a nose and to be compelled to hold it up like that. I would laugh if it were not so frightful.

Lorenzo. That is death, Ecco. But hide yourself, some one is coming.

> Ecco *conceals himself. Several* Peasants *enter and bow low at a little distance from the coffin, not venturing to come nearer.*

Lorenzo. [*Impressively*] Duke Lorenzo, open your heart and return to life for a moment. Your good peasants have come to bid you farewell. Come nearer, my friends. Duke Lorenzo in his lifetime was a kind master, and now that he is dead he will not harm you. Draw nearer.

> *The* Peasants *approach, though it is apparent that they are still afraid.*

First Peasant. God forgive you, Duke Lorenzo, as I forgive you. Many a time you and your hunters have trampled down my fields of grain, and what the hoofs of your horses left untouched your kind overseer took for himself, depriving me and my family of bread. Yet you were a good master, and I pray God to forgive you your sins.

LORENZO. [*To the one lying in the coffin*] Quiet, sir, quiet. I understand how it is with you: you cannot hear unmoved this bitter truth about your evil deeds. But do not forget that you are dead. Lie quiet, sir, lie quiet.

A PEASANT WOMAN. May God forgive you, Duke Lorenzo, as I forgive you. You took my little daughter from me for your ducal pleasure, and she was ruined. But you were young and handsome, and you were a good master to us. I pray God to forgive you your sins. [*She weeps.*

LORENZO. [*To the one lying in the coffin*] Quiet, sir, quiet. I remember how you loved the blue corn-flowers amid the ripened grain. Does not this remind you of some one's blue eyes, of some one's golden hair?

SECOND PEASANT. On the very eve of your departure for Palestine, Duke Lorenzo, to deliver the Holy Sepulchre, my son was killed in your service. A poor service you rendered to the Lord, Duke Lorenzo, and you shall have no forgiveness either on earth or in heaven.

LORENZO. [*Setting his teeth*] Did you hear, sir? [*To the* PEASANTS] Return in peace to your homes, my friends. Duke Lorenzo has heard you, and he will humbly bear your every word to the throne of the Almighty.

The PEASANTS *withdraw.*

LORENZO. [*To the one lying in the coffin*] Lorenzo, insane Lorenzo, what have you done to me?

Enter SIGNOR CRISTOFORO, *slightly tipsy. He kneels unsteadily and for some time is silent.* ECCO *peeps from his hiding-place, then conceals himself again.*

LORENZO. He is listening, Signor Cristoforo.

CRISTOFORO. [*Swaying to and fro*] Duke di Spadaro! Lorenzo! Boy! How lonely I am without you. Forgive me, my poor boy. When your noble father and I returned from Palestine and you were born—and a little, red chap you were—I swore to your father that I would always protect you. And I have protected your wines. Pardon me, Lorenzo, but they drink like camels. To-day, however, having opened all the cellars, I knocked out the heads of the casks and slit all the skins and said: "Drink, you camels, you asses, you accursed sponges. I shall gird on my sword and go seek the murderer of my boy, of my dear Lorenzo."

[*He wipes his eyes with his fist and staggers to his feet.*

LORENZO. [*With dignity*] The Duke thanks you, Cristoforo. You are drunk, my old friend, but at your words the lips of his wound have opened and two crimson drops have welled up from the depths of his heart. They are yours, Cristoforo. Go.

CRISTOFORO *withdraws.* ECCO *creeps out, tinkling his bells.*

ECCO. Have you nothing for me, Lorenzo? Give me at least one little drop of blood from your heart. I am tired of being ill-tempered and deformed.

LORENZO. I will give you more than that, Ecco. Come and kiss me.

ECCO. I am afraid.

LORENZO. He loved you, little coward.

ECCO. If you were alive, Lorenzo, I should be glad to kiss you, but I am afraid of corpses. Why did you die, Lorenzo? It was unkind of you. [*He seats himself on the floor, curling his legs under him as if getting ready for a long and interesting conversation*] You see, Lorenzo, we must go away. You look upon me as a jester and do not take me seriously, but once when you were playing with me you touched me with your sword, and now I am just as much a knight as you are, Lorenzo. So listen to me. Cease being dead, take your sword, and we will go away together like two knights.

LORENZO. [*Smiling*] Whither, my doughty knight?

ECCO. To the Lord God! [*With growing animation*] He knows you, Lorenzo, and, as for me, you will tell him that I am your brother, a little hunchback. And when he has sanctified our swords— Oh, oh, Lorenzo, there come your ruffians! I am afraid; I will hide myself.

He conceals himself. A band of drunken, boisterous SERVANTS *come in, reeling and jostling one another. Several keep their hats on.*

LORENZO. [*Angrily*] Off with your hats, you villains! Lie quiet, sir, lie quiet.

PIETRO. Bah! He's already beginning to stink. Whoever wishes can go and kiss his hand. I won't.

MARIO. I'd rather kiss Donna Francesca. Of all the ladies I have seen, she pleases me best. You see, gentlemen, the inclination is inherited; my uncle kissed Duke Lorenzo's mother, so I want to kiss his wife.

Laughter.

LORENZO. I implore you, sir, be quiet. I see how the black blood surges in your wound, but it is another's blood, Lorenzo.

MANUCCI. Pietro, you have stolen one of my golden spurs. To-morrow I shall flay you for it.

PIETRO. And I'll lop off your nose.

LORENZO. Away with you, you villains; be off!

He half draws his sword. The SERVANTS *look about in fright.*

PIETRO. Did you say that, Mario?

Mario. Sh! I heard the voice of the dead Duke, old Henry. Let's be off.

Manucci. I'll have the hide of you yet.

Mario. Come, let's be off.

They go out.

Lorenzo. [*To the one lying in the coffin, contemptuously*] And these, sir, are your servants, to whom you intrusted your castle, your treasures, and your wife, the beautiful Donna Francesca. Let us have no charges of disloyalty or treason, unhappy Duke. Do not insult me with lying evasions nor stain your honourable grave with sin. [*Greatly agitated*] Be calm, sir, be calm. I hear Donna Francesca coming. I recognise her step, and I implore you, sir, in the name of God, lie quiet. Summon your strength, sir.

> *Silence. The mournful notes of the requiem from behind the wall grow louder.* Lorenzo, *bending forward and laying his hand upon his heart, awaits the appearance of* Donna Francesca. *She enters alone, clad in deep mourning. She kneels. Silence. During the following scene* Ecco *comes partly out from the black drapery and weeps bitterly, softly tinkling his bells.*

Lorenzo. [*Unable to control himself*] I love you, Francesca.

Francesca. [*In a low voice*] I love you, Lorenzo.

Lorenzo. [*Sadly*] But you see that I am dead, Francesca.

Francesca. To me, Lorenzo, you will always be alive.

Lorenzo. [*Sadly*] You will forget me, Donna Francesca.

Francesca. I shall never forget you, Lorenzo.

Lorenzo. [*Sadly*] You are young, Donna Francesca.

Francesca. In a single night my heart has grown old, Lorenzo.

Lorenzo. [*Sadly*] Your face is beautiful, Donna Francesca. [*Gently reproachful*] Bitter tears have not dulled the bright gleam of your eyes, O Donna Francesca! Bitter tears have not washed the delicate roses from your cheeks, O Donna Francesca! Your black mourning does not conceal the grace and beauty of your form, O Donna Francesca, O Donna Francesca!

FRANCESCA. The light has gone out of my eyes, Lorenzo. My face has withered as a leaf withers at the cruel touch of the sirocco, and my form is bowed to the earth in bitter and overwhelming grief.

LORENZO. That is not true, Francesca.

FRANCESCA. I swear it, Lorenzo.

LORENZO. [*His voice trembling*] Lie still, sir, lie still. I see how your heart heaves, Lorenzo. I see how your tortured heart quivers at the pitiless words of love, and I pity you, Lorenzo. Go, Donna Francesca. Leave me with my dead friend. Your beautiful grief tears at our hearts, and I implore you in the name of God to leave us.

DONNA FRANCESCA *weeps*.

LORENZO. [*In an agony of grief*] O Donna Francesca! O my love! O light of my youth! [*Covering his face with his hands, he weeps silently*] Draw nearer, Francesca. Kiss him. I will not look.

FRANCESCA, *sobbing convulsively, kisses the dead* LORENZO.

LORENZO. [*Covering his face with his hands*] Kiss him more ardently, Donna Francesca, for you will never see him again. Kiss him more ardently. God placed a sword in my hand, and with it I punished the insane Lorenzo. But still he was a knight. He was a Knight of the Holy Ghost, Francesca. And now leave us.

Ecco, *frightened, conceals himself.* DONNA FRANCESCA, *in tears, descends from the dais, kneels again, and*

*withdraws. Silence. The last mournful strains of
the funeral dirge are heard.*

LORENZO. [*To the one lying in the coffin*] I thank you for obeying my behest and lying quiet. I saw how hard it was for you, and again I thank you, Lorenzo. Now we are alone—now and for ever. Let us go, Lorenzo; let us go into the unknown future.

The stage is suddenly dark.

Curtain.

SCENE V

The same hall as in Scene I. It is toward evening. Through the half-open window mountain peaks are seen glowing in the last rays of the setting sun. A fire burns in the fireplace. A number of candles are burning, but two SERVANTS, *moving along the wall, continue to light others. Silence.*

PIETRO. Why have they ordered so many candles to be lighted? Is any one expected to-day? I have heard nothing of it.

MARIO. Hold your tongue, stupid. You talk as if you didn't know.

PIETRO. [*Gruffly*] How should I know? They call me in when they need me, but as soon as anything goes wrong they shout: "Begone!"

MARIO. Everybody knows. The townspeople of Spadaro came up to the castle to-day. So they know, too. You're the only one that hasn't heard.

PIETRO. I don't care to hear. Only tell me, why so many lights?

MARIO. Because Duke Lorenzo has so ordered.

PIETRO. But why did he so order?

MARIO. Because to-day Duke Lorenzo is expecting guests.

PIETRO. Well, I said myself that there were to be guests. You might have told me in the beginning.

MARIO. [*Sighing*] You're stupid, Pietro. There will be no guests to-day. It's only that Lorenzo expects them.

PIETRO. How can he expect them if they are not coming?

MARIO. He imagines that they are coming. Do you understand, stupidity? He only imagines it. Probably you, when you are drunk, imagine things also. Why did you cry out yesterday in your drunken sleep?

PIETRO. I dreamt that Signor Cristoforo was beating me with his cane.

MARIO. There, now. You see, don't you?

PIETRO. Well, is the Duke, then, drunk? [*He laughs.*

    PETRUCCIO, *the overseer, enters.*

PETRUCCIO. Lively, now, you lazybones, lively! You, there, Pietro, what are you yawning about?

MARIO. My dear Signor Petruccio, you are so wise that even Signor Cristoforo listens to you. Explain to this fool what has happened to our Duke.

PETRUCCIO. That, my fine fellows, is none of your affair.

PIETRO. There, you've got your explanation. Which of us is the fool now?

PETRUCCIO. [*Gazing at the ceiling*] Both of you. The Duke is simply indisposed. He has delirium.

PIETRO. But why so many lights?

PETRUCCIO. Because— Clear out!

    Enter CRISTOFORO. PIETRO *bows low before him.*

PETRUCCIO. Good evening, Signor.

CRISTOFORO. Ah, Petruccio, Petruccio, when will you become thin so that you may contain less wine?

PETRUCCIO. If I become any thinner I shall be like a long drain-pipe, which, letting everything flow through, contains naught.

CRISTOFORO. [*Threatening him with his finger*] Take care, take care, Signor Overseer. [*Sighs*] Well, drink all you like, Petruccio. No one is left to save the wine for. Poor Lorenzo, poor Lorenzo! Little did I think, when we returned from Palestine with his father, that so horrible a fate was in store for the proud family of the Dukes of Spadaro. What has come over him? Where hovers his immortal soul? I looked him in the eyes to-day with a gaze that might have pierced the head of a wine-cask, but he merely smiled at me and, in a voice that would have brought tears to the eyes of a heathen Turk, said gently: "Who are you? I don't know you. Take off your mask, Signor."

PETRUCCIO. Indeed, indeed! but that is amazing, Signor Cristoforo.

CRISTOFORO. "My boy," I said to him, "Duke Lorenzo, just stop and think. If this were a mask, then what a horrible mask I should be wearing." [*Wiping away his tears*] "My boy," I said, "Duke Lorenzo, just touch with your finger this scar that I received in defending the Holy Sepulchre. Do masks have such scars?"

MARIO. Really, really! Holy Virgin!

CRISTOFORO. And Lorenzo put his finger on the scar and said: "What a wretched mask, Signor; it is apparently made of two pieces sewed together." Poor Lorenzo, poor Lorenzo!

> ECCO *appears and shrinks into a corner, making himself as small as possible. He sighs deeply.*

PETRUCCIO. You see that Ecco, too, is sad, Signor. It's an ill thing in a house when the jester takes to sighing like a half-frozen dog. Man cannot live without laughter, Signor Cristoforo. When laughter dies the man dies too. Laugh,

ACT II. SC. V THE BLACK MASKERS

Ecco. Even if you utter no word, at least laugh, and you will cheer my soul.

Ecco. [*With a deep sigh*] I cannot, Signor Petruccio.

Cristoforo. Don't you find my queer moustachios very amusing?

Ecco. [*With a deep sigh*] Very, Signor Cristoforo.

Cristoforo. Then why don't you laugh?

Ecco. I cannot, Signor Cristoforo.

Petruccio. There, you see for yourself. Laughter is dead. Poor Lorenzo!

Cristoforo. Yes. Poor Lorenzo!

All the candles are now lighted and the Servants *withdraw.*

Petruccio. Mario, go tell Donna Francesca that the candles are lighted and all is in readiness—for the reception of the guests.

Cristoforo. What guests, pray, can there be, Signor Overseer?

Petruccio. [*With a gesture of despair*] And you, Pietro, go and see that the drawbridge is lowered.

Cristoforo. What for?

Petruccio. The Duke so ordered.

Cristoforo. Lorenzo? Why do you take orders from him?

Petruccio. If, Signor Cristoforo, you had heard his voice and seen his gesture of command, you would have obeyed him too.

Cristoforo. I? Never.

Ecco. You would have obeyed, Signor Cristoforo, as I obeyed. What was I? A little, malicious dwarf found in the castle moat. When he so willed, I became his laughter. And what shall I now become? It is not for you to judge, gentlemen. I shall be whatever my master, Lorenzo, bids.

PETRUCCIO. His tears?
ECCO. [*Sighing*] No.
CRISTOFORO. His fears?
ECCO. [*Sighing*] No, his fire. I was his tears. I do not know, Signor Cristoforo, if I was his fears, but now I shall become his fire. He said to me, as he said to you: "Who are you, sir? I do not know you. Take off your mask." And I fell to weeping, gentlemen, and replied: "Very well, Lorenzo. If you bid me, I will take off my mask."
CRISTOFORO. No, Ecco, you were better when you smiled.

> *Enter* SIGNORA FRANCESCA *with her suite of ladies and gentlemen. They move silently and sadly about the hall, embarrassed by its emptiness and the brilliant lights.*

A GENTLEMAN. [*In a low voice*] It seems an eternity since I kissed you last, Leonora.
LEONORA. And it will be an eternity before you kiss me again, sir.
THE GENTLEMAN. How cruel you are, my goddess. As if one eternity were not enough.
DONNA FRANCESCA. I beg of you, ladies and gentlemen, to do me a favour. You are no doubt aware that the Duke, my husband, is somewhat indisposed. He is expecting guests, though none are invited, and since he will probably assume, my dear friends, that you are his guests, I beg of you not to express surprise or alarm. The Duke's memory is somewhat impaired, so that he forgets even persons who are dear to him. Divert him, gently and cautiously, from his illusions. I count on your tact and kindness, my friends. Announce to Duke Lorenzo [*covering her face with her hands*] that the guests are arriving.
ECCO. [*Sighing*] I was his laughter. I was his tears. What shall I now become?   [*He rises and starts to go out.*

CRISTOFORO. Where are you going, Ecco?

ECCO. Where the will of my master may lead me.

FRANCESCA. Signor Petruccio, I trust that you have not forgotten the musicians. Have they learned the music that Duke Lorenzo composed for them?

PETRUCCIO. The musicians only await your instructions, madam.

VOICES. Silence! Silence! Duke Lorenzo! Duke Lorenzo!

> *On the brilliantly illuminated staircase appears* DUKE LORENZO. *He wears the same costume as at the ball, even to the torn doublet, which exposes the spot of blood on his breast over his heart. His face is very pale. He pauses and, looking radiantly about the brilliantly lighted hall, bows with an air of gracious hospitality.*

LORENZO. I am delighted to welcome you, my dear guests. From this moment my castle is at your disposal. I am merely your servant. Petruccio, is the roadway lighted?

PETRUCCIO. It is lighted, sir.

LORENZO. Do not forget, my friend, that the whole night is watching us. We will show it, sir, what is meant by a bright and living fire. [*He comes down*] What charming masks! I am happy, my friends, to be honoured by your presence. I am infinitely charmed by your inexhaustible cleverness and wit. Who are you, sir? I do not know you. Please remove your mask, that I may extend to you a friendly greeting.

CRISTOFORO. [*On the verge of tears*] It is I, Lorenzo. I am Cristoforo. Do you not know me?

LORENZO. [*With touching candour*] Why, how should I know you, sir, when you wear so frightful a mask? I knew a Signor Cristoforo. He was my friend from the cradle, and I loved him, but you I do not know. Remove your mask, my dear sir, I beseech you.

CRISTOFORO. I were better thrown to the dogs. I can bear no more.

FRANCESCA. Signor Cristoforo!

LORENZO. What ails the gentleman? Why does his mask change so oddly? I am extremely sorry, sir, and I should be infinitely pleased to learn who you are, but, pardon me, I do not recognise you. And who is this funny fat gentleman with the red nose? What a comical mask!

PETRUCCIO. I have just had the honour, sir— I am Petruccio, your overseer.

LORENZO. You mean you are wearing the mask of Petruccio.

PETRUCCIO. Yes, the mask of Petruccio.

LORENZO. [*Laughing*] A bad bargain, my dear sir. You made a poor choice. My overseer is a great rascal and a knave, and his red nose did not come from praying.

CRISTOFORO. My poor boy!

LORENZO. Ah, now I think of it, has any one of you gentlemen seen a masker in red entwined with a serpent that stings her in the heart? Right in this spot. They say [*laughing*]—they say [*laughing*] that it is my heart. A capital joke! As if every one did not know that Lorenzo, Duke of Spadaro, has no serpent in his heart.

ONE OF THE GUESTS. [*Incautiously*] You have wounded yourself on something, Duke Lorenzo. There is blood on your doublet.

LORENZO. [*Eagerly*] Oh, that? Thereby hangs a very strange story, gentlemen. It sounds like a fairy-tale. While I was in the tower, some stranger who had concealed his face under a hideous mask, extinguished the light, fell upon me in the darkness, and stabbed me in the back. As you see, gentlemen, the dagger entered under the left shoulder-blade and came out here at the breast. It was a skilful, if treacherous, stroke. My heart was pierced straight through.

FRANCESCA. [*Endeavouring to distract* LORENZO's *attention from the wound, which, throwing open his doublet, he eagerly displays*] Lorenzo!

LORENZO. See, ladies and gentlemen, what a master-stroke!

FRANCESCA. Look at me, Lorenzo. Why do you not smile upon me? I am sad when you do not smile. It is as if the sun had set for ever.

LORENZO. You are charming, Signora. I see only your supple figure and your tiny foot, but permit me, my divinity, to make so bold as to peep into your eyes— How they shine! Even through the openings of this ugly black mask I can see how beautiful they are. Who are you, madam? I do not know you.

FRANCESCA. God in heaven! Do you not recognise me, Lorenzo?

LORENZO. [*With the same touching candour as before*] Take off your mask, madam, I beseech you. Your question is a strange one. Take off your mask, madam, and I will greet you willingly and cordially. By your stature I should take you to be Signora Emilia; but no [*he shakes his head*], Signora Emilia is not so shapely. Who are you?

FRANCESCA. [*Weeping*] I am your wife, Lorenzo, your wife, Donna Francesca. My love, do you not remember that name—Francesca?

LORENZO. [*Knitting his brows*] Francesca? Did you say Francesca? Yes, that was my wife's name. True, that was my wife's name. But I have lost my wife. Have you not heard, madam? There is no Donna Francesca any more.

FRANCESCA. Remember how you loved me, Lorenzo. Look into my eyes. You said that among a thousand women you would recognise me by the eyes alone. Listen to my voice, Lorenzo—you are not looking at me.

LORENZO. [*Gently reproachful*] Your voice is tender and

kind, my lady. I hear in it the utterance of a virgin heart. Why do you inflict this painful jest upon me? You are cruel, my dear lady. You should not mock Lorenzo or twist the dagger in his bosom. I have lost my wife. Her name was Donna Francesca, and I have lost her.

FRANCESCA. If you do not believe me, my love, at least give me leave to touch with my lips your blood-stained wound. By the tenderness of her kiss you will recognise your Francesca.   [*She bends forward to kiss the wound.*

LORENZO. [*With an expression of extreme pain and horror, thrusting her away*] What are you about, madam? You are drinking my blood. Have mercy on me, I beg of you. You have fastened yourself on my heart and you are drinking my blood. You hurt me. Leave me, pray.

> DONNA FRANCESCA *weeps.* LORENZO, *shrinking from her with an expression of suffering and extreme terror, tries to cover the wound, but his hands tremble.*

LORENZO. [*Covering the wound and making an effort to smile*] A bitter jest, my friends. You saw how this vampire fastened herself upon my heart?

CRISTOFORO. [*Angrily*] You are crazy, Lorenzo, this is your wife!

A GENTLEMAN. He has insulted you, Donna Francesca.

FRANCESCA. [*Ceases weeping and speaks angrily*] It is you who insult him, sir! Lorenzo, Duke of Spadaro, cannot insult a woman even though he be insane.

LORENZO. [*To* PETRUCCIO, *in a low voice*] What is the trouble, Signor? What has disturbed this charming masker?

PETRUCCIO. I do not know.

FRANCESCA. Call the musicians, Petruccio.

LORENZO. [*Joyfully*] Yes, yes, call the musicians.

FRANCESCA. [*Tenderly*] I beg you to be attentive, my dear Lorenzo. Signor Romualdo will now sing for us the charming song that you dedicated to me in the bright days of our love.

LORENZO. You are jesting again, madam. I never loved you.

FRANCESCA. [*Greatly distressed*] Do not listen to him, my friends. I beg you to be seated, Duke, and, if you will permit me, I will sit beside you. Signor Romualdo, show the Duke the song which he wrote with his own hand in the bright days of our love. Do you recognise your handwriting, my dear Lorenzo?

LORENZO. [*Courteously*] Show it to me, Signor. Yes, that is my writing, and a capital joke it is, too. [*Glancing at* FRANCESCA] But here is written: "To my love, to my bride, the charming Donna Francesca." [*Suspiciously*] How did this sheet come into your hands, madam?

FRANCESCA. [*Hastily*] Signor Romualdo, I beg you to begin. We are listening.

Strains of soft and beautiful music flooded with sunshine and with the charm of youth and love.

ROMUALDO. [*Singing*] "My soul is an enchanted castle. I have lighted my castle with lights. I have lighted my castle with lights."

LORENZO. [*Searching his memory*] I seem to have heard those words before. Continue, Signor.

ROMUALDO. [*Singing*] "And the sun entered my charming castle. The black shadows fled affrighted, and an infinite joy, the revellings of a bright and happy soul, gave wings to my thoughts, O Donna Francesca! O Donna Francesca!"

LORENZO. The singer speaks falsely, my friends. I never wrote that.

ROMUALDO. [*Singing*] "And on wings of fancy my flaming spirit ascended to heaven. And on wings of fancy my flaming spirit ascended to heaven."

LORENZO. [*Rising and halting* ROMUALDO *with an angry gesture*] Stop, singer. Do not listen to him, my friends. He lies. He is deceiving you. I remember the words. Luigi, you villain, obey me. If you err even in a single note I will have you hanged to-morrow from the castle walls. Attention, ladies and gentlemen. [*Through the windows the far-off mountain tops stand out from the darkness as if touched by the red glow of sunset. From somewhere behind the* MUSICIANS *comes the wild music that was played at the ball, but no one hears it*] Right, right, Luigi. [*Singing*] "I, the insane Lorenzo, have lighted up my tower and hither will come those whom I invited not. And the lights in the tower will go out, and my soul will be shrouded in darkness and will rejoice in thee, my lord, my master, ruler of the world—Satan."

Cries of indignation and horror. Many, terrified, leave their places and crowd about the columns.

A VOICE. He is calling upon Satan.

SECOND VOICE. He says that Satan is lord of the world. Sacrilege! Sacrilege! Sacrilege!

CRISTOFORO. Awake, madman, you are the son of a crusader.

A LADY. [*To a gentleman*] Look, the sun is setting a second time!

VOICES. The sun! the sun! Look, the sun has appeared again!

CRISTOFORO. [*Stamping his foot*] Even though you are insane, even though you are my master, Duke Lorenzo, I throw down my gauntlet to you.

The others seize him. The light outside grows stronger and seems to be mixed with flame and blood. The mountains are no longer visible.

VOICES. Look! Look! See what is happening to the sky.

FRANCESCA. Duke Lorenzo is mad, Signor Cristoforo, and

cannot do you the honour of crossing swords with you, but in the name of his son, whom I bear in my bosom, I accept your challenge. [*She takes up the glove.*

VOICES. The Duchess expects a son. Donna Francesca expects a son. Poor Lorenzo! Poor Lorenzo!

LORENZO. [*Recovering from a profound reverie*] What has happened? I thought I heard the sound of a naked sword. Who dares to draw his sword in the presence of Duke Lorenzo? I showed you honour, my friends, and invited you to my festival. You outrage my hospitality.

VOICES. Look! Something has happened to the sky. There is a fire somewhere. See, the heavens are ablaze! What has happened? There is a fire somewhere.

LORENZO. [*Looking through the window and speaking with elation*] That is the beginning of my holiday, my friends. To our joyful banquet will come one more guest. I commend him to your attention. His eyes are fire, his bright locks are clouds of gilded smoke, his voice is the roar of the impetuous flame that devours stone, and his godlike visage is flame and fire and boundless, pellucid light. Such a masker, ladies and gentlemen, you have never seen!

The light outside becomes stronger. Frightened cries. Commotion. Voices.

VOICES. Satan! Satan! He calls on Satan. See, the heavens are on fire, the earth is ablaze! Save yourselves! He is summoning Satan.

LORENZO. [*Raising his voice*] Who dares to speak here the foul name of Satan? I thought I heard a strange song. Some madman, deserving of curses and death, called out in tremulous prayer the name of Satan.

CRISTOFORO. It was you, Lorenzo. You are the vassal of Satan.

LORENZO. I? Oh, no, sir. You imagined it. These

charming masks beget so many ridiculous misunderstandings. Some jester, assuming my voice and features, has long been deceiving you with a base falsehood.

CRISTOFORO. But you yourself called on the name of Satan.

LORENZO. Oh, no, my friends. [*Falling on his knees and speaking with solemnity*] He whom I have invited to my festival and who now deigns to appear—uncover, gentlemen—is the Lord God, the ruler of heaven and earth. On your knees, knights and ladies. [*Nearly all kneel. Several weep. Low exclamations:* "God in heaven! God in heaven!" Ecco, *the jester, rushes in, all ablaze, and runs frantically about the hall. The* SERVANTS, *shouting, pursue him*] To me, Ecco; I am here.

MARIO. Seize the villain. He has fired the tower.

PIETRO. He has strewn fire about, and the castle is burning on all sides. Save yourselves, ladies and gentlemen. In a moment the fire will seize upon the staircase.

MANUCCI. We must kill him. Strike him! Strike him!

LORENZO. [*To whose knees presses the blazing and almost blinded jester*] Back! Who dares touch the messenger of God? Back, sirs! [*He draws his sword.*

ECCO. [*Trembling*] Is it you, Lorenzo? I am blinded. The fire has burned out my eyes. Do not drive me away, Lorenzo.

LORENZO. Brother, you shall greet our great Master along with me.

> *The window-glass crashes. Above appear tongues of flame commingled with volumes of black smoke. Panic and flight. Shouts.*

VOICES. Save yourselves! Save yourselves!

FRANCESCA. Fly, Lorenzo, fly!

LORENZO. Your heart has stopped beating, Ecco. Hold fast to life for at least a moment. He comes, Ecco.

ACT II. SC. V **THE BLACK MASKERS** 63

ECCO. [*Trembling*] Is he coming? Do you see him?

LORENZO. I hear him, Ecco.

ECCO. I am dying, Lorenzo. But do you tell him that I am your little brother.

LORENZO. I will tell him.

ECCO. [*Growing calmer*] You know—they gave me some bells—I forgot to cut them off—I am dying, Lorenzo.

FRANCESCA. Fly, Lorenzo!

CRISTOFORO. Do you not see, madam, that he is mad? If you will permit me, I will take him in my arms, as I did when he was a child, and carry him away.

He approaches LORENZO, *but, encountering the point of his sword, steps back.*

LORENZO. Stand back, sir.

CRISTOFORO. Well, come on, then. [*He draws his sword.*

FRANCESCA. Go, Signor Cristoforo. Do not dare to touch that which belongs to God alone.

CRISTOFORO. Well, be it so. But I shall not leave without you, my lady.

FRANCESCA. I leave you, Lorenzo. In the name of your unborn son, I leave you and renounce the happiness of dying with you. But I shall tell your son, Lorenzo, how the Almighty called you to himself, and he will bless your name.

The fire breaks through everywhere.

CRISTOFORO. Quick, madam, quick!

FRANCESCA. Farewell, my Lorenzo; farewell, my beloved; farewell.

LORENZO. Farewell, Signora. I regret that you wear a mask. Your voice and your words remind me of Donna Francesca. I beg of you, Signora, bear to her my last farewell.

FRANCESCA. Farewell.

CRISTOFORO. Come! Away! Away!

He takes DONNA FRANCESCA *in his arms and, making his way through the clouds of smoke, carries her out. There remain only* LORENZO *and* ECCO, *the latter having fallen at* LORENZO'S *feet. The fire spreads over everything. Outside the broken windows and the ruined doors, in the midst of the black volumes of smoke, appear the* BLACK MASKERS. *One can see their ineffectual efforts to enter the castle, their silent struggle with the fire, which lightly and buoyantly tosses them back. Again and again they rush forward, only to fall back writhing with pain.*

LORENZO. Up, Ecco, the Lord is coming. [*He touches* ECCO, *but the jester falls lifeless from him. The flames now completely surround them. The* BLACK MASKERS *have disappeared. The crackling and roaring of the triumphant fire is heard. Solemnly*] I greet thee, O Lord. While I still lay in the cradle my father touched me with his sword and consecrated me a Knight of the Holy Ghost. Do thou touch me, O Lord, if I am worthy of thy accolade. [*Falling on his knees*] But this truth, I aver, O Lord, is known to all people in the world: Lorenzo, Duke of Spadaro, has no serpent in his heart!

[*The fire envelops him. Everything falls in ruins.*

Curtain.

THE LIFE OF MAN
A DRAMA IN FIVE ACTS
With a Prologue

THE LIFE OF MAN
PROLOGUE

A BEING IN GREY *called* HE *speaks of the life of* MAN. *The scene resembles a large, rectangular, perfectly empty room, without doors or windows. Everything in it is grey and misty and of uniform colour: grey walls, grey ceiling, grey floor. From an invisible source comes a feeble, diffused light, which, also grey, is monotonous, uniform, and unreal, casting neither shadows nor spots of light. The* BEING IN GREY *comes gradually into view against the background of the wall, with which he has been merged. He wears a broad, shapeless, grey robe which vaguely outlines the contours of a large body. Upon his head there is a heavy grey scarf which throws a dark shadow over the upper part of his face. The eyes are not visible. That which is visible—the cheek-bones, nose, and sharp chin—is massive and solid, as if hewn from grey stone. The lips are firmly compressed. Slightly raising his head, he begins to speak in a firm, cold voice, calm and passionless, like a hired lector reading with severe indifference the Book of Fate:*

"Look and listen, ye who have come hither for mirth and laughter. Lo, there will pass before you all the life of Man, with its dark beginning and its dark end. Hitherto non-existent, mysteriously hidden in infinite time, without thought or feeling, utterly unknown, he will mysteriously break through the barriers of non-existence and with a cry will announce the beginning of his brief life. In the night of nonexistence will blaze up a candle, lighted by an unseen hand. This is the life of Man. Behold its flame. It is the life of Man.

"After birth he will take on the image and the name of man, and in all respects he will be like other people who already live on the earth, and their cruel fate will be his fate, and his cruel fate will be the fate of all people. Irresistibly dragged on by time, he will tread inevitably all the steps of human life, upward to its climax and downward to its end. Limited in vision, he will not see the step to which his unsure foot is already raising him. Limited in knowledge, he will never know what the coming day or hour or moment is bringing to him. And in his blind ignorance, worn by apprehension, harassed by hopes and fears, he will complete submissively the iron round of destiny.

"Behold him, a happy youth. See how brightly the candle burns. The icy wind blowing from infinite space puffs and whirls about, causing the flame to flutter. The candle, however, burns clearly and brightly, though the wax is melting, consumed by the fire. The wax is melting.

"Lo, he is a happy husband and father. Yet look! How dim and strange the candle glimmers, as if the flame were a yellowing leaf, as if the flame were shivering and shielding itself from the cold. For the wax is melting, consumed by the fire. The wax is melting.

"Lo, now he is an old man, feeble and sick. The path of life has been trodden to its end and now the dark abyss has taken its place, but he still presses on with tottering foot. The livid flame, bending toward the earth, flutters feebly, trembles and sinks, trembles and sinks, and quietly goes out.

"Thus Man will die. Coming from the night he will return to the night. Bereft of thought, bereft of feeling, unknown to all, he will perish utterly, vanishing without trace into infinity. And I, whom men call He, will be the faithful companion of Man throughout all the days of his life and in all his pathways. Unseen by Man and his companions, I shall unfailingly be near him both in his waking and in his sleeping hours; when he prays and when he curses; in hours of joy when his free and bold spirit soars high; in hours of depression and sorrow when his weary soul is overshadowed by deathlike gloom and the blood in the heart is chilled; in hours of victory and defeat; in the hours of heroic struggle with the inevitable I shall be with him—I shall be with him.

"And ye who have come hither for mirth, ye who are doomed to die, look and listen. Lo, the swiftly flowing life of Man will pass before you, with its sorrows and its joys, like a far-off, thin reflection."

The BEING IN GREY *ceases, and in the silence the light goes out and darkness envelops him and the grey, empty room.*

Curtain.

ACT I

THE BIRTH OF MAN AND THE SUFFERINGS OF THE MOTHER

A profound darkness within which nothing moves. Then there can be dimly perceived the outlines of a large, high room and the grey silhouettes of OLD WOMEN *in strange garments who resemble a troop of grey, hiding mice. In low voices and with laughter to and fro the* OLD WOMEN *converse.*

CONVERSATION OF THE OLD WOMEN

What I should like to know is whether our friend will have a son or a daughter.

What difference does that make to you?

I like boys.

And I like girls. They always stay at home and wait until you come to them.

But do you like to make calls?

Subdued laughter.

He knows.

He knows.

Silence.

Our friend would like a girl. She says that boys are too rough, that they are venturesome and seek dangers. When they are still quite small they like to climb tall trees and swim in deep water, and often they fall, and often they drown. And when they become men they start wars and kill each other.

She thinks that girls don't drown, but I have seen many drowned girls just the same, and they were like all drowned people—wet and greenish.

She thinks stones don't kill girls.

Poor thing! Childbirth is so hard for her. Here we have been sitting for sixteen hours and she is still crying. At first she cried loud so that her shrieks hurt your ears, then lower, and now she only gasps and moans.

The doctor says she'll die.

No, the doctor says the child will die and that she will be left alive.

Why do they have children? It is so painful.

Why do they die? That is still more painful.

Subdued laughter.

Yes, they bear children and they die.

And again bear children.

They laugh. The low cry of the suffering woman is heard.

It has begun again.

Her voice has come back. That's good.

That's good.

The poor husband! He is so distracted that he is funny to look at. At first he was glad that he was to have a child, and said that he wanted a boy. He thought that his son would be an ambassador or a general. But now he doesn't want anything, neither a boy nor a girl, and he only runs about distractedly and weeps.

When her throes begin, he strains too, and flushes.

When they sent him to the drug store for some medicine he rode up and down past the store for two hours and could not remember what he wanted. So he came back.

Subdued laughter. The crying again becomes louder and then dies away. Silence.

What has happened to her? Perhaps she is already dead.

No, in that case we should hear weeping. The doctor would run out and begin to talk nonsense, and they would bring out her husband unconscious, and we should have our hands full. No, she is not dead.

Then why are we sitting here?

Ask Him. How should we know?

He won't tell.

He won't tell. He tells nothing.

He drives us here and there. He rouses us from our beds and makes us watch, and then it turns out that there was no need of our coming.

We came of our own accord. Didn't we come of our own accord? You must be fair to Him. There, she is crying again. Aren't you satisfied?

Are *you?*

I am saying nothing. I am saying nothing and waiting.

How kind-hearted you are!

Laughter. The cries become louder.

How she screams! What pain she suffers! You know these pains? They are like having the entrails torn out.

We have all borne children.

How strange her voice is! I don't recognise the voice of our friend. It is usually soft and gentle.

But this cry is more like the howl of a wild animal. One can feel the night in this cry.

One can feel in it hopelessness and terror. It is like an endless dark forest.

One can feel solitude and anguish in it. Can it be that no one is with her? Why are there no other voices but this wild cry?

There *are* voices, but you cannot hear them. Haven't you noticed how solitary a human shriek always is? All may be talking, but you don't hear them; yet if only one shrieks, it is as if everything were silent and listening.

I once heard a man shriek. A wagon had crushed his foot. Though the street was full of people, it was as if he were actually the only one there.

But this is more frightful.

Rather say louder.

More prolonged, I should say.

No, it is more frightful. You can feel death in it.

Well, you could feel death there, too. The man died.

Stop quarrelling! Isn't it all the same to you?

Silence. A scream.

How strange is a human cry! When you yourself cry out in agony, you do not notice how strange it is—how strange it is!

I can't picture to myself the mouth that is uttering those sounds. Can it be the mouth of a woman? I cannot picture it.

But you can feel that it is all distorted.

The sound seems to be born in some abyss. Now it is like the cry of a drowning person. Listen, she's gasping.

Some heavy thing is lying on her chest.

Some one is stifling her.

The cries cease.

At last she has ceased. One gets tired of it. The cry is so monotonous and ugly.

Oh, you want beauty here, too, do you?

Subdued laughter.

Sh! Is He here?

I don't know.

I think He is.

He doesn't like laughter.

They say He laughs himself.

Who ever saw Him laugh? You are simply repeating rumours. They tell so many lies about Him.

He will hear us. Let's be serious.

Subdued laughter.

Just the same, I'd like to know whether it will be a boy or a girl.

Yes, it's interesting to know with whom you have to deal.

I'd rather it would be still-born.

How kind-hearted!

No more than you.

Well, I want him to become a general.

Laughter.

You laugh too much. I don't like it.

And I don't like your glumness.

Stop quarrelling! Stop quarrelling! We are all of us both mirthful and gloomy. Let each one be as she likes.

Silence.

They are awfully queer when they are born. Funny little things!

And so self-satisfied.

And they demand so much. I don't like them. They begin right off to cry and to insist, as if everything ought to be ready for them. Even before they can see they know that there is a breast and milk and insist on having them. And then they demand that they be laid to sleep. And then they demand to be rocked and to have their little red backs gently patted. I like them better when they die. Then they are less insistent. They straighten themselves out and don't ask to be rocked.

Yes, they are very funny. I like to wash them when they are born.

I like to wash them when they are dead.

Stop quarrelling! Stop quarrelling! Every one shall have

her own way. One will wash the child when it is born, another when it dies.

But why do they think they have a right to make demands as soon as they are born? I don't like that.

They don't think. It is the stomach that insists.

They are always insisting.

Because no one gives them what they need.

Subdued laughter. The cries in the next room are renewed.

She is crying out again.

Animals have an easier time.

And they die easier and live easier. I have a cat. If you could only see how fat and contented she is!

And I have a dog; and every day I say to her: "You are going to die." But she only grins and cheerfully wags her tail.

Well, they are animals.

Well, these are people.

Laughter.

Either she is dying or the crisis has come. In this cry you can feel the limit of her strength.

You can feel the rolling eyes.

And the cold sweat on her forehead.

They listen.

The child is being born.

No, the mother is dying.

The cries are suddenly broken off.

I tell you——

THE BEING IN GREY. [*Speaks in a clear and powerful voice*] Silence! Man is born.

Almost simultaneously with his words the cry of a child is heard, and the candle in his hand flames up. The tall candle burns with a feeble, uncertain light, but gradually the flame becomes stronger. The corner in which the BEING IN GREY *stands motionless is darker than the other corners, and the yellow flame of the candle illuminates the square chin, the firmly compressed lips, and the large, bony cheeks. The upper part of the face is hidden by the heavy folds of the scarf. He is somewhat larger than an ordinary man.*

The candle, long and thick, is set in a candlestick of antique workmanship. Against the green bronze his hand stands out grey and firm, with long, slender fingers.

As it grows slowly brighter there emerge from the darkness the outlines of the room and the figures of five hunchbacked OLD WOMEN *in outlandish robes. The room is high and rectangular, with smooth, uniformly tinted walls. In front of the spectator, and also at his right, are two tall windows with eight panes of glass each and without curtains. The night looks in through the windows. Along the wall stand chairs with tall, straight backs.*

THE OLD WOMEN. [*Hastily*] Hear them running about. They are coming here.

How light it is! Let's go.

Look, the candle is tall and the flame is bright.

Let's go; let's go. Quick!

But we'll come back!

But we'll come back!

They laugh softly and in the dim light glide out with odd, zigzag movements, interchanging laughter. On their departure the light, though it grows stronger, remains comparatively dull, lifeless, and cold. The corner in which the BEING IN GREY *stands motionless with the burning candle, is darker than the other corners.*

Enter the DOCTOR, *in a white surgeon's coat, and the* FATHER OF MAN. *The face of the latter wears a happy though wearied expression. Under his eyes are blue circles. His cheeks are hollow and his hair is dishevelled. He is carelessly dressed. The* DOCTOR *has a learned air.*

DOCTOR. Up to the last moment I was uncertain whether your wife would remain among the living or not. I used all my skill and knowledge, but our science means little if nature does not come to our aid. I am much agitated. How my pulse beats even now! Although I have helped so many children to come into the world, to this day I cannot avoid this excitement. But you are not listening to me, sir!

FATHER OF MAN. I am listening, but I hear nothing. Her cries are still ringing in my ears, and I find it hard to understand. Poor woman! How she suffered! Fool that I was, insane, to wish for children! I now renounce this criminal desire.

DOCTOR. But you will call me when the next one is born.

FATHER. That will never be. I am ashamed to say it, but at this moment I hate the child for whom she suffered so. I have not even seen it. What is it like?

DOCTOR. It is a strong, well-nourished boy and, if I am not mistaken, resembles you.

FATHER. Resembles me? How delightful! Now I begin to love it. I have always wished to have a son like myself. Did you notice whether his nose is like mine?

DOCTOR. Yes, his nose and his eyes.

FATHER. His eyes, too? Oh, fine! I will pay you more than I agreed.

DOCTOR. I must have an extra fee for the use of the forceps.

FATHER. [*Turning to the corner where* HE *stands motionless*] O God, I thank thee for fulfilling my desire and giving me a son like to myself. I thank thee that my wife did not die and that the child lives. And I beg thee so to order his life that he may grow up strong and healthy and be wise and honest, and that he may never bring grief upon us—upon me and his mother. If thou doest this, I shall ever believe in thee and go to church. And now I dearly love my son.

Enter the KINSPEOPLE, *six in number. One is an unusually tall, elderly lady with double chin and small, haughty eyes. She is extremely dignified and proud. An elderly gentleman in spectacles, her husband, is very tall and so excessively thin that his garments hang about him. He has a pointed beard like a goat's, and his hair, smooth as though pomaded, reaches to his shoulders. He seems timid, but nevertheless has an air of wisdom. In his hand he carries a low, black silk hat. A young girl, their daughter, has a silly, turned-up nose, blinking eyes, and open mouth. There is also a thin lady with an extremely uncomfortable and sour expression. She holds in her hands a handkerchief with which she frequently wipes her mouth. Two* YOUNG MEN, *exactly alike, display unusually tall collars which hold their necks stiffly up. They have smoothly plastered hair and wear an expression of perplexity and absent-mindedness. In each character all of the qualities mentioned are carried to an extreme.*

ELDERLY LADY. Allow me, dear brother, to congratulate you on the birth of your son. [*She kisses him.*

GENTLEMAN. Allow me, my dear kinsman, to congratulate you heartily on the birth of a son so long expected.

[*He kisses him.*

THE OTHERS. Allow us, dear kinsman, to congratulate you on the birth of your son.

[*They kiss him. The* DOCTOR *withdraws.*

FATHER. [*Deeply moved*] I thank you, I thank you. You are all so very good. You are such kind and affectionate people. I love you dearly. Heretofore I had my doubts, and I thought that you, dear sister, were somewhat absorbed in yourself and your virtues, and that you, dear brother-in-law, were somewhat pedantic, and of the others I thought that they were cool toward me and only came for the dinner. But now I see that I was wrong. I am extremely happy. A son is born to me. A son is born to me like myself, and aside from that I see here so many good people who love me.
[*They kiss.*

YOUNG GIRL. What are you going to name your son, dear uncle? I should so like him to have a beautiful, poetic name. With a man so much depends on the name.

ELDERLY LADY. I should like the name to be simple and substantial. People with beautiful names are always rattle-brained and rarely succeed in life.

ELDERLY GENTLEMAN. I think, dear brother-in-law, that you ought to name your son for some one of your older kinsmen. That has the effect of continuing and strengthening the family.

FATHER. Yes, my wife and I have already thought about it, but we could not come to a decision. So many new ideas and interests come with the birth of a child.

ELDERLY LADY. It rounds out one's life.

ELDERLY GENTLEMAN. It gives life a beautiful purpose. In bringing up a child, by saving him from the errors of which we ourselves were the victims, by storing his mind from our own rich experience, we produce a better man and slowly but surely move toward the final goal of existence—perfection.

FATHER. You are perfectly right, my dear brother-in-law. When I was small I was very fond of torturing animals, and this developed in me a strain of harshness. I shall not allow my son to torture animals. Even after I was grown up, I frequently made mistakes in friendship and love. I selected unworthy friends and perfidious women. I will explain to my son——

The DOCTOR *enters and speaks in a loud voice.*

DOCTOR. Sir, your wife is very ill. She wishes to see you.

FATHER. O heavens! [*He goes out with the* DOCTOR.

The KINSPEOPLE *seat themselves in a semicircle and for some time maintain an impressive silence. In the corner the* BEING IN GREY *stands motionless with his stony face turned toward them.*

CONVERSATION OF THE KINSPEOPLE

Can it be, my dear wife, that our kinswoman will die?

No, I hardly think so.

Having very little patience, she makes too much of her suffering. All women bear children, and no one dies. I myself have borne six children.

But she screamed so, mamma.

Yes, her face was flushed with screaming. I noticed that.

That was not from screaming. That was because she had to strain so. You don't understand these things. My face has been flushed, too, but I never screamed. A friend of ours, the wife of the engineer, recently bore a child, and she hardly cried at all.

Yes, I know. My brother is needlessly worried. One must be firmer and take a calmer view of things. I am afraid that when he comes to bring up the child he will make him visionary and dissolute.

He lacks will-power. Though he has little money, yet he loans to untrustworthy people.

Do you know how much the child's linen cost?

Oh, don't mention it! My brother's folly is so trying. He and I have had arguments on this subject before.

They say storks bring babies. Storks!

The YOUNG GENTLEMEN *snicker.*

Stop your silliness. I have had five children, and, thank God, I am no stork.

The YOUNG GENTLEMEN *snicker again, and the* ELDERLY LADY *looks at them severely for a long time.*

You should understand that this is a superstition. Children are born in a perfectly natural manner, on strictly scientific principles.

They live in another flat now.

Who?

The engineer and his wife. Their old quarters turned out to be very damp and cold. They complained several times to the landlord, but he paid no attention.

In my opinion a small, warm flat is better than a large, damp one. In a damp flat one might die of catarrh or rheumatism.

One of my acquaintances has a very damp flat.

And one of mine, too—very damp.

There are so many damp flats nowadays.

But tell me, please—I have been wanting to ask you for ever so long—how can grease spots be taken out of white cloth?

Wool?

No, silk.

Cries of the child in the other room.

Take a small piece of clean ice and rub the place where the spot is real hard, and when you have rubbed it real hard take a hot iron and smooth it.

You don't say so! How simple! But I have heard that borax water is better.

No, borax water is good only for dark cloth. For white cloth ice is the best thing.

I say, may one smoke here? I somehow never happened to think whether it would be proper to smoke where a child had just been born.

Nor I. How strange! At funerals I know it is quite improper to smoke, but here——

What nonsense! Of course you can smoke.

However, smoking is in general a bad habit. You are still a very young man. I should advise you to attend to your health. In the course of one's life so many occasions arise when one needs one's health.

But tobacco is stimulating.

Believe me, it is a very unwholesome stimulation. When I was young and thoughtless I used tobacco to excess.

Oh, mamma, how it cries! How it cries, mamma! Does it want milk?

The YOUNG GENTLEMEN *snicker. The* ELDERLY LADY *looks severely at them.*

Curtain.

ACT II

LOVE AND POVERTY

The scene is flooded with a bright, warm light. A large, very high, and very bare room. The walls, of a light rose-colour, are perfectly smooth and covered in places with a fantastic and beautiful lacework of damp lines and spots. In the right wall are two tall windows, each with eight panes of glass and without curtains. The night looks in through them. There are two wretched beds, two chairs, and a table without a spread. On the table stands a beautiful bouquet of wild flowers and a half-broken pitcher containing water.
In one corner, which is darker than the other corners, stands the BEING IN GREY. *The candle in his hand is diminished by one third, but the white flame is still bright and high and throws brilliant spots of light on his stony face and chin.*
The NEIGHBOURS *enter, dressed in bright, gay garments. Their hands are filled with flowers and grasses and fresh, green branches of oak and birch. They move about the room. Their faces are open, cheerful, and kindly.*

CONVERSATION OF THE NEIGHBOURS

How poor they are! Just see, they haven't a single extra chair!

Nor curtains at the windows——

Nor pictures on the walls——

How poor they are! See, they have nothing to eat but stale bread——

And nothing but water to drink—cold water from a well.

And they have no extra clothing, either. She always wears her rose-coloured dress with the open neck, which makes her look like a young girl.

And he always wears his blouse and his fantastic necktie, which makes him look like an artist and causes all the dogs to bark angrily at him——

And offends all proper people.

Dogs hate shabby people. Only yesterday I saw three dogs attack him, and as he drove them away with a stick he cried: "Don't you dare touch my trousers! They are my only trousers!" Then he laughed, and the dogs showed their teeth and rushed at him and howled with anger.

And to-day I saw two very respectable-looking people, a gentleman and a lady, who, frightened by him, crossed to the other side of the street. "He will ask us for money in a minute," said the gentleman. "He will kill us!" piped the lady. So they crossed the road, looking about and holding their pockets. But he shook his head and laughed.

He is so cheerful.

They are always laughing.

And singing.

It's he who sings; she dances.

In her rose-coloured dress with the open neck.

It is a delight to look at them. They are so young and radiant.

But I am so sorry for them. They are hungry. Just think of it, hungry!

Yes, that is so. They used to have much furniture and clothing, but they have sold all and now they have nothing left to sell.

I remember she had beautiful earrings, and she sold them to buy bread.

And he had a handsome, black dress coat—his wedding-coat—and he sold it.

They have nothing left but their wedding-rings. How poor they are!

That's nothing, that's nothing! I was young myself once and I know what it means.

What's that you say, grandfather?

That's nothing, that's nothing!

Just see, merely thinking of them makes grandfather want to sing!

And dance!

Laughter.

He is so kind. He made my boy a bow and arrows.

And she wept with me when my daughter was sick.

He helped me mend my broken fence. He is a strong young fellow.

It's a delight to have such good neighbours. Their youth warms our cold age; their light-heartedness drives away our cares.

But their room is like a prison: it's so empty.

No, it is like a temple: it's so bright.

See, they have flowers on the table. She gathered them while she was walking about the fields in her rose-coloured dress with the open neck. Here are lilies-of-the-valley. The dew is not yet dry on them.

And here is flaming scarlet lychnis.

And here are violets.

And here is just green grass.

Don't touch them, girls! Don't touch the flowers! Don't drop them on the floor—her kisses are on them. Don't breathe on them with your breath—her breath is on them. Don't touch them, girls! Don't touch the flowers!

He will come and see the flowers.

He will take the kisses.
He will drink in her breath——
How poor they are! Yet how happy!
Let's go. Let's go away.
But has none of us brought anything for our dear neighbours? That would be too bad!
I have brought a piece of fragrant, warm bread and a bottle of milk. [*She puts it on the window-sill.*
And I have brought some soft, tender grass. When it is scattered about the floor, the room is like a blossoming meadow and smells like spring.
[*She strews the grass on the floor.*
And I have brought flowers. [*Strewing them.*
And we have brought branches of birch and oak with green leaves. When the walls are hung with them the room will look like a cheery, green forest.
They decorate the room, filling the dark windows and covering the bare, rose-coloured walls with leaves.
I have brought a fine cigar. It is a very cheap one, but it is strong and fragrant and will bring delightful dreams.
[*He lays it on the window-sill.*
I have brought a rose-coloured ribbon. When you tie it in your hair it makes you gay and beautiful. My lover gave it to me, but I have many ribbons and she has none at all. [*She lays it on the window-sill.*
How about you, grandfather? Haven't you brought something?
Nothing. Nothing. I brought only my cough, and they don't need that, do they, neighbour?
No more than my crutches— Say, girls, who needs my crutches?
Do you remember, neighbour——?
And do you remember, neighbour——?

THE LIFE OF MAN

Let's go to bed, neighbour. It's already late.

They sigh and go out, one of them coughing and the other's crutches clattering on the floor.

Let's go! Let's go!

God grant them happiness. They are such good neighbours.

God grant they may always be healthy and cheerful, and love each other, and that no ugly black cat may ever run between them.

And that the young man may find work. It is bad when a man has no work.

They withdraw, and immediately the WIFE OF MAN *enters, very beautiful, graceful, tender, and delicate, with flowers in her splendid, half-dishevelled hair. She is very sad. She seats herself in a chair and, laying her hands on her knees, speaks sorrowfully, her face toward the audience:*

I have just been to town and have been hunting. I don't know what I was hunting for. We are so poor. We have nothing. It is very hard for us to live. We need money, but I don't know how to get it. If you ask it of people, they won't give it; and I haven't the strength to take it from them. I was hunting for work, but no one gave me any work. They all said to me: "There are so many people and so little work." I kept my eyes on the road, thinking perhaps some rich people might have dropped a purse, but either they did not drop one or some one more fortunate than I had already picked it up. And I am so sad. You see my husband will soon come back from his hunt for work, tired out and hungry, and what can I give him except my kisses? He cannot satisfy his hunger with kisses, can he? I feel so sad. I'd like to cry.

I can go without eating for a long time. I don't mind it. But he cannot. He has a large body which demands nourishment, and when he has not eaten for some time he becomes pitifully pale, and sick, and irritable. He scolds me, but afterward he kisses me and asks me not to be angry. But I never get angry, because I love him so. I am only sad.

My husband is a very talented architect; I even think he is a genius. His parents died very early and left him an orphan. For some time after the death of his parents his relatives supported him, but since he was always very independent in character and brusque, and often said unpleasant things, and did not express his gratitude, they cast him off. But he continued to study, supporting himself by giving lessons, and often going hungry. And so he finished his course in the university. He was often hungry, my poor husband. Now he is an architect and makes designs of beautiful buildings, but no one will buy them, and lots of stupid folks even laugh at them. In order to get on one must have either a patron or a stroke of good fortune. But he has neither patron nor good fortune. He goes about, hunting for some opportunity or, perhaps, looking on the ground for money as I did. He is still very young and is simple as a child.

Of course, fortune will come to us sometime, but when? Meanwhile, it is very hard to keep alive. When we were married we had a little dowry, but we quickly used it up. We always went to the theatre and ate candy. He still is hopeful, but I sometimes lose all hope and weep by myself. My heart sinks when I think that he may be here at any moment and again find nothing except my poor kisses.

O God, be a kind and merciful father to us! Thou hast so much of everything—bread and work and money. Thy earth is so rich. It bears fruits and grain in the fields and covers the meadows with flowers. From its dark depths it yields up gold and beautiful precious stones. And thy sun is so warm, and there is so much quiet joy in thy pensive stars. Give us a little bread from thy bounty—even a very little —only so much as thou givest thy birds, that my dear, good husband may not be hungry; a little warmth, that he may not be cold, and a little work, that he may proudly hold up his beautiful head. And pray do not be angry with my husband because he scolds and laughs, or even sings and makes me dance. He is so young and so light-hearted.

Now that I have prayed I feel better and again I have hope.

Really, why should God not give when we pray like this? I will go out and hunt a little. Perhaps some one has dropped a purse or a sparkling diamond. [*She goes out.*

THE BEING IN GREY. She does not know that her wish is already fulfilled. She does not know that this morning two men, in a costly house, bending over a design of Man's, eagerly scanned it and were delighted with it. All day they have been hunting in vain for Man. Wealth has been seeking him, as he is seeking wealth, and to-morrow morning when the neighbours go away to work, an automobile will come to the house and two gentlemen, bowing low, will enter the bare room and bring wealth and fame. But they do not know this—neither he nor she. Thus fortune and happiness come to Man, and thus they leave him.

> MAN *and his* WIFE *enter.* MAN *has a handsome, proud head, with flashing eyes and high forehead. His dark brows divide above his nose and spread like two bold wings. His wavy, black hair is carelessly thrown back. His low, soft, white collar displays a shapely neck and part of his chest. His movements are light and swift like those of a young animal, but the attitudes he takes are peculiar to* MAN *alone; they are masterful, free, and proud.*

MAN. Again nothing. Pretty soon I shall go to bed and lie there all day long. The people that need me can come and find me. I shall not go to find them. To-morrow I am going to lie abed.

WIFE. Are you tired?

MAN. Yes, I am tired and hungry. Like Homer's hero, I could eat a whole bull, and here I have to be satisfied with a crust of stale bread. Do you know that a man cannot always live on bread alone? I want to gnaw, tear, bite!

WIFE. I am so sorry for you, dear.

MAN. Yes, I am sorry for myself, but that doesn't satisfy my hunger. To-day I stood for a whole hour in front of a lunch-room and gazed on the chickens and the tarts and the sausages, just as people view works of art. And oh, the signs! They can paint ham so exquisitely that one could eat it, iron and all.

WIFE. I like ham, too.

MAN. Is there anybody who doesn't like ham? Do you like lobsters?

WIFE. Yes, I do.

MAN. Oh, what a lobster I saw! Though he was only a painted lobster, he was more handsome than a live one. Red as a cardinal, majestic, severe. One might kneel to him for a blessing. I think that I could eat two such cardinals and a carp thrown in.

WIFE. [*Sadly*] Didn't you notice my flowers?

MAN. Flowers! Can you eat flowers?

WIFE. You don't love me.

MAN *kisses her.*

MAN. Forgive me, but really I am so hungry. See how my hands shake. I haven't strength enough to throw a stone at a dog.

WIFE *kisses his hand.*

WIFE. Poor dear!

MAN. How did these leaves come to be on the floor? How sweet they smell! Did you put them there, too?

WIFE. No; probably it was our neighbours.

MAN. Our neighbours are dear people. Strange that with so many good people in the world a man can die of hunger. Why is it?

WIFE. You have become gloomy; you frown. Do you see anything?

MAN. Yes, before me, across my humorous fancies, a hideous image of poverty glided stealthily and rose up yonder in the corner. Do you see her? The pitiful, outstretched hands—like those of a child lost in the woods—the voice appealing to the silence of the human desert: "Help me!" No one hears. "Help me, I am dying!" No one hears. Look, Wife, look! Look! The black shadows, trembling, float apart like wraiths of black smoke from the long, dreadful chimney that leads down to hell. Look! I, too, am in the midst of them!

WIFE. You terrify me. I cannot look in that dark corner. Did you see all this on the street?

MAN. Yes, I saw it all on the street, and soon it will be here.

WIFE. No, God will not let it come to us.

MAN. Why does he let it come to others?

WIFE. We are better than others. We are good people. We do not anger him in any way.

MAN. Do you think so? But I often scold.

WIFE. You are not wicked.

MAN. Yes, I am wicked, I am wicked. When I walk along the street and look at the things that are not ours, I grow boar's tusks. Oh, how much money there is that is not mine! Listen, my dear little Wife. This evening I was walking in the park, in that lovely park where the roads are straight as arrows and the beautiful beech-trees are like crowned kings——

WIFE. And I was walking along the city streets, where there were stores and stores, such beautiful stores——

MAN. Well-dressed people with canes passed me, and I thought: "I have none of that."

WIFE. Handsomely gowned women in well-fitting boots which make the foot charming, in rustling silk skirts, and in elegant hats from beneath which their eyes sparkled mysteriously, passed by me, and I thought: "I have no fine hat, I have no silk skirt."

MAN. One awkward fellow shouldered me aside, but I showed him my tusks and he slunk cowardly behind the others.

WIFE. A finely dressed lady jostled me, but I was so embarrassed that I did not even look at her.

MAN. Riders swept by me on proud and fiery horses, but I have no horse.

WIFE. And such diamonds were in her ears! I wanted to kiss them.

MAN. Red and green automobiles glided by noiselessly like phantoms with blazing eyes, and people were sitting in them laughing and listlessly glancing from side to side, but I have no automobile.

WIFE. And I have neither diamonds nor emeralds—not even a pure white pearl.

MAN. On the shore of the lake glittered a luxurious restaurant with lights like the kingdom of heaven, and people were eating there. There were high officials in dress suits, and angels with white wings who distributed beer and bread and butter, and people were eating and drinking. Oh, I want to eat, little Wife, I want to eat!

WIFE. My dear boy, if you keep running about you will increase your hunger. Come, sit down, and I will sit on your knees. Now, take a paper and draw a beautiful, beautiful building.

MAN. But my genius is hungry, too, and it won't sketch anything but edible landscapes. For a long time my palaces have looked like big dumplings stuffed with fat and my churches like sausages. But there are tears in your eyes. What is the matter, little Wife?

WIFE. I am sad because I cannot help you.

MAN. You make me ashamed. Though I am a strong man, intelligent, talented, and healthy, I can do nothing, while my little wife, my fairy, weeps because she is not strong enough to help me. When woman weeps, man is disgraced. I am ashamed of myself.

WIFE. You are not to blame if people cannot appreciate you.

MAN. I am blushing to the tips of my ears. I feel like a child whose ears have been pulled. You, too, are hungry, and I, selfish creature that I am, had not noticed it. I'm a brute.

WIFE. But, my dear, I am not hungry.

MAN. It is disgraceful, cowardly. That rude fellow who jostled me was right. He saw that I was nothing but a fat pig, a boar with sharp tusks and a stupid head.

WIFE. If you are going to scold yourself so unfairly, I shall begin to cry again.

MAN. No, no. Don't cry. When I see tears in your eyes I am always terrified. I am afraid of those bright crystal drops. It is as if they were shed not by you but by some one else, some frightful being. I won't let you cry. True, we have nothing, we are miserably poor; but I will tell you what we are going to have. I will charm you with a beautiful story. I will enwreath you, my queen, with rose-coloured dreams.

WIFE. You need not fear. You are strong and talented and you will succeed. The moment of depression will pass, and a divine inspiration will again throw its halo over your proud head.

MAN. [*Assumes an attitude of bold and proud defiance, and, throwing an oak spray into the corner where the* UNKNOWN *stands, he cries*] Ho, you, whatever your name may be—Destiny, the Devil, Life—I throw down the gauntlet to you. I challenge you to battle. The faint-hearted bend their knees before your mysterious power. Your stony face fills them with horror. In your silence they hear the coming to birth of misfortune and its ominous approach. But I am bold and strong, and I challenge you to battle. Let our swords flash, let our shields ring, let the blows fall on our heads —blows that will shake the earth. Come forth to battle!

WIFE. [*Approaching and standing close behind his left shoulder, speaks earnestly*] Bolder, my dear, still bolder!

MAN. To your inertness, sinister being, I oppose my bold, living strength. To your gloom I oppose my clear and ringing laughter. Parry the blows! Against your stony face, in which there is no light of reason, I hurl the projectile of my glowing thought. You have a heart of stone that knows no pity. Stand aside! or I will pour into it the seething poison of rebellion. The black cloud of your fierce wrath has darkened the sun. We will light up the darkness with our swords. Ho! Parry the blows!

WIFE. Bolder, still bolder! Behind you stands your armour-bearer, my proud knight.

MAN. If I conquer, I shall sing songs which all the world will echo; and if I fall dumbly under your blows, then I shall think only of how I may rise again and rush to battle. There are weak spots in my armour, I know, but, though covered with wounds and dripping with crimson blood, I shall yet gather strength to cry: "You have not yet conquered, malicious enemy of mankind!"

WIFE. Bolder, my knight! I will wash your wounds with my tears. With my kisses I will stanch the flow of your crimson blood.

MAN. And dying on the field of battle as brave men do, I shall mar your brute pleasure with one last cry: "I have conquered!" I have conquered, malicious foe, for with my last breath I shall refuse to acknowledge your supremacy.

WIFE. Bolder, my knight, bolder! I will die with you.

MAN. Ho! Come forth to battle! Let our swords flash, let our shields ring, let the blows fall on our heads, blows that will shake the earth. Ho! Come forth!

For some time MAN *and his* WIFE *remain in the same attitudes, and then they turn to each other and kiss.*

MAN. Thus we shall share life together, my little Wife, shall we not? Let life blink like an owl blinded by the sunshine, we will force her to smile.

WIFE. And to dance to our songs—we two together!

MAN. We two. You are a good wife and a faithful friend. You are a brave little woman, and as long as you and I are together nothing can terrify us. What is poverty? To-day we are poor, and to-morrow we are rich.

WIFE. And what is hunger? To-day we are hungry, to-morrow we are filled.

MAN. Oh, you think so, do you? Perhaps, but it will take a great deal to fill me. My hunger isn't easily satisfied. Do you think this will be plenty? In the morning, tea, coffee, chocolate—take your choice—and then, after that, breakfast—three courses—then lunch, then dinner, then——

WIFE. Lots of fruit. I am so fond of fruit.

MAN. All right. I will buy it in baskets in the market. It is cheaper there and fresher; though, to be sure, we shall have our own orchard.

WIFE. But we have no land.

MAN. I'll buy some. For a long time I have wanted a little plat of my own, and, by the way, I'll build a house on it after my own design. I'll show the rascals what sort of architect I am!

WIFE. I want to live in Italy, right by the sea, in a white-marble villa set in a grove of lemon-trees and cypresses; and I'd like some white-marble steps leading straight down to the blue water.

MAN. I see. Good! But besides that I mean to build a castle in Norway among the mountains: far below, the fiord; high up on the steep cliff, the castle.—Haven't we any paper? No matter, the wall will do. Here is the fiord. Do you see it?

WIFE. Yes—how lovely!

MAN. The water is sparkling and deep. Here it reflects the tender, green grass and there the red and black and brown stone. And see, here in the opening, right where this spot is, a touch of deep-blue sky and a quiet, white cloud——

WIFE. Look! A white boat is reflected in the water. It is like two white swans, breast to breast.

MAN. And see, here the mountain rises from the cheerful green meadows and forests, and, as it mounts, becomes more and more gloomy, more and more severe. There are sharp cliffs, black shadows, precipices, ragged clouds——

WIFE. It is like a ruined fortress.

MAN. And see, on this fortress, right on this spot here in the centre, I will build a castle fit for an emperor.

WIFE. How cold it is there, and how the wind blows!

MAN. Oh, but I'll have thick stone walls, and there will

be huge windows of one large pane, and on winter nights, when the blizzard rages and the fiord is roaring below, we will draw the curtains and kindle a fire in the huge fireplace. There will be great andirons on which will burn whole logs —whole forests of pitchy pine.

WIFE. Oh! How warm!

MAN. And see, how still! Everywhere rugs, and lots and lots of books which radiate silent yet living warmth and comfort, and we two together. Outside roars the storm, but here we are together in front of the fireplace on a white bear's skin. You say, "Shall we take a peek at what's going on outside?" and I say, "Very well," and we go to the largest window and draw the curtain. Heavens! What's that?

WIFE. Whirling snow!

MAN. It sweeps by like white horses. Look, myriads of little frightened spirits, white with terror, seeking refuge from the night! And the whistling and the roaring——

WIFE. Oh, it's cold! I am shivering.

MAN. Quick! Back to the fire. Here, give me my ancestral beaker. No, not that one, the gold one that the vikings drank from. Fill it with golden wine—more—let the fiery liquid rise to the very brim. There's a chamois roasting on the spit. Bring it here; I will eat it. Quick, or I will eat you instead! I'm starved! I'm hungry as the devil!

WIFE. There, now; they've brought it. What are you going to do next?

MAN. What next? Why, eat it, of course. What else could be next? But what are you doing with my head, little Wife?

WIFE. I am the Goddess of Fame. I have twined for you a wreath of the oak leaves which our neighbours strewed, and I am crowning you. Fame has come—glorious fame!

[*She puts the wreath on his head.*

MAN. Yes, fame, loud-voiced, echoing fame. Look at the wall. See, here I go, and do you know who is by my side?

WIFE. Why, that's me.

MAN. See, people are bowing to us. They are whispering about us. They are pointing at us. See that respectable-looking old gentleman who falls a-weeping and says: "Blessed is our native land to have such children!" See that pale young man who is looking at us. Fame has smiled upon him, also. By this time I have built the People's Palace of which our whole country is so proud.

WIFE. You are my glorious hero! The oak wreath becomes you, but a laurel wreath would be even better.

Man. Look! look! Here are representatives of the city where I was born coming to me. They bow low and say: "Our city is proud of the honour——"

WIFE. Oh!

MAN. What's the matter?

WIFE. I have found a bottle of milk!

MAN. Impossible!

WIFE. And bread—soft, fragrant bread—and a cigar!

MAN. Impossible! You have made a mistake. What you think is milk is only the dampness from this accursed wall.

WIFE. No, indeed!

MAN. A cigar! Cigars don't grow on window-sills. They sell them at ridiculously high prices in the stores. This is probably just a black, broken twig.

WIFE. But, do look! Ah, now I understand! Our dear neighbours brought it.

MAN. Neighbours! Upon my word, they are angels. And even if the devil himself had brought these things—bring them here quick, my little wife. [*The* WIFE *of* MAN *sits on his knees and they eat, she breaking the pieces of bread and putting them in his mouth while he gives her milk from the bottle*] It looks like cream.

WIFE. No, it's milk. Chew your bread more slowly or you'll choke yourself.

MAN. Give me the crust. It is so nicely browned.

WIFE. There, didn't I tell you you would choke yourself?

MAN. It's all right; got it down.

WIFE. The milk's running down my neck and my chin—oh, it tickles!

MAN. Here, let me drink it up. [*He drinks it off her neck and chin*] We mustn't waste a drop.

WIFE. What a mischief you are!

MAN. There, everything's eaten up. That was quick work. Everything that is good comes soon to an end. This bottle must have a double bottom. To look at it you would think it was deeper. What cheats these bottle makers are! [*He lights the cigar, and assumes an attitude of supreme contentment. She ties the rose-coloured ribbon in her hair, using the black window for a mirror*] This seems to be an expensive cigar. It is very fragrant and strong. I am always going to smoke that kind.

WIFE. You're not looking at me.

MAN. Yes, I am. I see everything. I see the ribbon, and I see that you want me to kiss your throat.

WIFE. I won't let you, you silly man. You can smoke your cigar if you like, but as for my throat——

MAN. What, isn't it mine? The deuce! That is a violation of property rights. [*She runs away. He catches her and kisses her*] There, the right is restored, and now, my little Wife, dance for me. Just imagine that this is a magnificent, luxurious, astounding, miraculously beautiful palace.

WIFE. I've imagined it.

MAN. Now imagine that you are the queen of the ball.

WIFE. It's done.

MAN. And that marquises and counts and lord mayors are asking you to dance with them, but you decline them all and select the—what do you call him—the fellow in tights? Oh, yes, the prince. Why! What's the matter?

WIFE. I don't like princes.

MAN. Oh, that's it! Well, what sort do you like?

WIFE. I like talented artists.

MAN. Good! Here's your artist. Oh, heavens! Look at you there flirting with empty space! Oh, woman!

WIFE. But I was just imagining.

MAN. Oh, all right. Now imagine a wonderful orchestra. See, here's a big Turkish drum—boom, boom, boom!

[*He pounds his fist on the table in imitation of a drum.*

WIFE. My dear, it is only in a circus that they call the crowd together with a drum; in a palace——

MAN. Oh, the deuce! Stop the picture. Now imagine again. Listen! The singing violins are pouring forth their melody, and here sounds the tender voice of a flute. Listen! The fat bass viol is booming like a beetle— [MAN, *wearing the oak wreath, sits and strikes up the tune of the dance, beating time with the palms of his hands. The tune is the same as that which is played in the following act, at the ball of* MAN. *The* WIFE *dances gracefully*] Ah, my little gazelle!

WIFE. I am the queen of the ball.

The song and dance become more and more lively. Presently MAN *gets up, begins to dance where he stands, and finally seizes his* WIFE *and dances with her, the oak wreath slipping to one side.*

The BEING IN GREY *watches them with indifference, holding in his stony hand the brightly blazing candle.*

Curtain.

ACT III

A BALL AT THE HOUSE OF MAN

A ball is going on in the great hall of the spacious house of MAN. The hall is a large, high, rectangular room with perfectly smooth white walls and ceiling and a light-coloured floor. There is a certain lack of harmony in the parts, the doors, for example, being disproportionately small as compared with the windows. In consequence of this the hall produces a strange and somewhat irritating impression, an impression of something inharmonious, something incomprehensible, something non-essential and intrusive. The room is pervaded by a chilly whiteness, its monotony being broken only by a row of windows along the rear wall. These are very high, reaching almost to the ceiling, and are close together. Through them the night shows dark and gloomy. Not a single gleam of light, not one bright spot, is visible in the empty caverns enclosed by the frames. The wealth of MAN is shown by the abundance of gilding. There are gilded chairs and very broad gilded frames on the pictures. These are the only furnishings and the only decoration of the immense room. The hall is illuminated by three chandeliers in circular form, with electric lights set at wide intervals around them. Near the ceiling the room is very bright, but lower down the light is noticeably less, so that the walls appear greyish.

The ball at the house of MAN is at its height. An orchestra of three is playing. The musicians bear a striking resemblance to their instruments. Thus, the one with a fiddle resembles a fiddle, having a very thin neck and a small head with a topknot drooping to one side. His body is somewhat bent. Over his shoulder, underneath the fiddle, a handkerchief is carefully spread. The flutist resembles a flute. He is very long and very thin, with a long-drawn-out face and long-stretched-out thin legs. The one with the bass viol resembles a bass viol. He is short, has drooping shoulders, is very broad below the waist, and wears broad pantaloons. They play with an infinite painstaking which is very conspicuous. They keep time by shaking their heads and swaying their bodies. The tune during the entire ball is always the same. It is a rather brief polka of two musical phrases, with dancing notes, cheerful but very empty. The instruments are slightly out of tune with each other and consequently there is between them, as well as between the successive notes, a strange incoherence and, as it were, empty spaces.

The young girls and young men, all of them very handsome, well-formed, and elegant, are dancing a dreamy dance.

In contrast to the loud and jerky sounds of the music, their dancing is very smooth, silent, and light. During the first musical phrase they circle about; during the second one they separate and reunite gracefully and a trifle artificially.

Along the wall on the gilded chairs sit the GUESTS *in rigid, formal attitudes. They move stiffly, scarcely turning their heads. They also speak stiffly—there is no whispering nor smiling—without looking at each other, and utter, jerkily and abruptly, only such words as are given in the text. Their hands seem to be broken at the wrist and hang in an attitude of stupid pride. In spite of the extreme and sharply marked differences in their faces, they all wear a similar expression of self-satisfaction, arrogance, and sodden reverence for the wealth of* MAN.

The girls who are dancing wear white gowns: the men are dressed in black. The GUESTS *wear black, white, and bright yellow.*

In the corner nearest the spectators, which is darker than the other corners, the BEING IN GREY, *called* HE, *stands motionless. The candle in his hand is already reduced by two thirds and burns with a vivid yellow flame, throwing yellow patches of light on his stony face and chin.*

CONVERSATION OF THE GUESTS

I must observe that it is a very great honour to be a guest at the ball of Man.

You might add that this honour is bestowed upon very few. The whole city tried to get invitations, but very few received them. My husband, my children, and I are all very proud of the honour which highly respected Man has bestowed upon us.

I even feel a sort of pity for those who couldn't come. All night they will lie awake from envy and to-morrow they will slander us and tell how people are bored at the balls of Man.

They have never seen this brilliancy.

You might add, this amazing wealth and luxury.

Precisely what I mean: this charming, care-free joy. If this is not joy, then I should like to know where joy is.

Enough. You cannot convince people who are tortured by envy. They will tell us that we did not sit on gilded chairs—that there were no gilded chairs at all!

And they will say that they were just ordinary, cheap chairs bought at a second-hand store.

And that there was no electric light but simply tallow candles.

Why not say candle-ends?

Or wretched night-lamps. Oh, slander! slander!

And they will barefacedly deny that there are gilded cornices in the house of Man.

And that the pictures have broad, gilded frames. It seems to me I can hear the gold jingling.

You see it glitter; that is sufficient, I should say.

I have rarely had opportunity to enjoy such music as one hears at the balls of Man,—this divine harmony which wafts the soul to higher spheres.

Music ought to be good when it costs so much. You should not forget that this is the best orchestra in the city and that it plays on the most élite occasions.

This music runs in your head for a long time. It certainly takes the ear captive. My children on returning from the balls of Man hum the tune for a long time.

I sometimes think I hear it on the street. I look around, but there are no musicians and no music.

And I hear it in my dreams.

I must say that I am particularly pleased with the painstaking manner in which the musicians play. They understand how much money they have received for their music, and they wish to give some return for it. That is perfectly proper.

They work as hard as if they had themselves entered into their instruments.

Rather say their instruments have entered into them.

How costly!

How gorgeous!

How brilliant!

How costly!

> *For some time, in different parts of the room, the two expressions,* "How costly!" "How gorgeous!" *are repeated abruptly with a sound resembling a bark.*

Aside from this hall Man has fifteen magnificent rooms, and I have seen them all. The dining-room has a fireplace so huge that whole logs can be burned in it. There are magnificent reception-rooms and a boudoir. The sleeping chambers are roomy, and above the heads of the beds— just think of it—are baldachins!

Yes, isn't it amazing! Baldachins!

Do you hear? Baldachins!

Allow me to continue. For his little son there is a beautiful, bright room finished in wood of a golden yellow colour. The sun seems always to shine in it.

Oh, such a charming boy! He has curls like the sun's rays.

Quite true. When you look at him you involuntarily think: What, has the sun risen?

When you look at his eyes you think: Why, autumn is over and the blue sky has come again!

Man loves his son passionately. For horseback riding he has bought him a pony, a cunning, snow-white pony. My children——

Allow me to continue, I beg of you. Have I spoken yet of the bath?

No, no!

Ah, the bath!

Yes, the bath!

Yes, hot water all the time. Then, farther on, is the library of Man himself, and there you see nothing but books, books, books! They say he is very wise, and you could infer that from his books.

I once saw the garden. Have you seen it?

No, I have not had that pleasure.

Well, I saw the garden, and I must say that it charmed me. Just picture to yourself lawns of emerald, incredibly smooth, and down the middle two paths sprinkled with fine, red sand. Then flowers, even palms!

Even palms?

Yes, even palms. And all the trees are clipped, too, some of them like pyramids, others like green columns. And there is a fountain, and shining, coloured globes, and in the midst of the green grass stand little plaster-of-paris gnomes and mountain goats.

How costly!

How gorgeous!

For some time they repeat abruptly: "How costly!" "How gorgeous!"

Man did me the honour of showing me his stables and his carriage houses, and I expressed my unqualified approval of his horses and carriages. In particular, the automobile made a peculiarly deep impression on me.

And—think of it!—he has as many as seven servants! A man and woman cook, two chambermaids, gardeners, the——

You left out the coachman.

Oh, yes, of course, the coachman.

And they themselves do nothing. They are so important.

Everybody agrees that it is a great honour to be a guest of Man.

But don't you find this music somewhat monotonous?

Dear me, no! I don't find it so, and I am surprised that you do. Don't you see what kind of musicians these are?

As for me, I should like to hear this music all my life long. There is something in it which thrills me.

And me.

And me.

Under its spell how delightful it is to give oneself up to sweet dreams of bliss——

And to be wafted away in them to the interstellar spheres.

How fine!

How costly!

How gorgeous! [*They repeat these exclamations.*

I see a commotion at the doors yonder. Man will now pass through the hall with his Wife.

The musicians are becoming completely exhausted.

There they are!

They're coming! Look, they're coming!

> *In the low, double door at the right appear* MAN, *his* WIFE, *his* FRIENDS, *and his* ENEMIES. *They cross the hall diagonally, going toward the door at the left. The dancers, continuing to dance, divide their ranks and make way for them. The musicians play with desperate loudness and discordancy.*
>
> MAN *has grown much older. In his long hair and his beard are traces of grey, but his face is manly and handsome, and he walks with a calm dignity and a certain reserve. He looks straight ahead, apparently not observing those about him. His* WIFE, *leaning on his*

arm, is still beautiful, though she also has grown older. She, too, apparently does not see what is going on about her, and with a somewhat strange, almost fixed, gaze looks straight before her. Both are richly dressed.

Immediately behind MAN *walk his* FRIENDS. *They all resemble one another, having noble faces, open, high foreheads, and honest eyes. As they walk proudly forward with chests thrown out and with confident, firm tread, they look from side to side condescendingly and with a slightly scornful air. All have white roses in their buttonholes.*

A little way behind them come the ENEMIES *of* MAN. *They also resemble one another closely. All have depraved faces, low foreheads, and long, monkey-like arms. They walk restlessly, jostling each other, crouching, hiding behind each other, and casting sidewise under their brows keen, sneaking, envious glances. In their buttonholes are yellow roses.*

In this manner they pass slowly, without speaking, across the hall. The sound of the footsteps, the music, and the exclamations of the guests produce a confused and markedly inharmonious noise.

THE GUESTS

There they are! There they are! What an honour!
How handsome he is!
What a manly face!
Look! Look!
He doesn't even glance at us.
He doesn't see us.
We are his guests.
What an honour! What an honour!

And she, look, look!
How beautiful she is!
How proud!
Do just look at her diamonds!
Diamonds! Diamonds!
Pearls! Pearls!
Rubies!
How gorgeous! What an honour!
Honour! Honour! Honour!
 [*They repeat the exclamations.*
And there come the Friends of Man.
Look, look! There are the Friends of Man.
What noble faces!
What a proud walk!
They bask in his fame.
How they love him!
How faithful they are to him!
What an honour to be a Friend of Man!
They look upon everything as if it were their own.
They feel at home here.
What an honour!
Honour! Honour! Honour!
 [*They repeat the exclamations.*
And there are the Enemies of Man!
Look, look! The Enemies of Man!
They walk like whipped dogs.
Man has humbled them.
He has muzzled them.
See how they wag their tails.
How they slink along!
They jostle each other.
Ha! Ha! Ha! Ha! [*They laugh.*

What villainous faces!
What greedy glances!
Cowards!
Envious!
They are afraid to look at us.
They feel that we are at home here.
We must scare them still more.
Man will be grateful to us.
Scare them, scare them!
Boo! Boo!

> *They shout at the* ENEMIES *of* MAN, *intermingling the cry "Boo! Boo!" with their laughter. The* ENEMIES *crowd together and cast timid but sharp glances from side to side.*

They are going out! They are going out!
What an honour!
They are going out!
Boo! Boo! Ha! Ha! Ha!
They're gone! They're gone! They're gone!

> *The procession disappears through the door at the left. A period of silence follows. The music is not so loud, and the dancers gradually fill the room.*

Where did they go?

I think they went to the dining-room. They are serving dinner there.

Probably they will soon invite us, too. Don't you see some one looking for us?

Indeed, it's high time. If one dines too late, one sleeps badly.

For my part, I dine very early.

A late dinner sits heavy on the stomach.

The music is still playing.

And they are still dancing. I am surprised that they can hold out so long.

How gorgeous!

How sumptuous!

Do you know for how many persons the table is laid?

I had no chance to count. The butler came in and I took occasion to withdraw.

It cannot be that they have forgotten us.

Man, you see, is so proud, and we are so petty.

Your remark is quite uncalled for. My husband says that we show him honour by attending. We are quite wealthy ourselves.

If you take into account the reputation of his Wife——

Don't you see some one looking for us? Perhaps they are looking for us in the other rooms.

How rich——

In my opinion one may quite easily become rich by handling other people's money carelessly.

Silence! Only his Enemies say that——

Well, there are perfectly honourable people among them. I am bound to say that my husband——

Dear me! How late it is!

Apparently there is some misunderstanding. I cannot believe that they have simply forgotten us.

Evidently you understand life and human nature very little, if you think that.

I am surprised. We ourselves are quite wealthy——

I think I heard some one calling us.

You only imagined it. No one called us, and, to speak frankly, I don't understand why we have come to a house with such a reputation. One should be careful in the selection of one's associates.

A Servant in Livery *appears at the door.*

Servant. Man and his Wife invite their honoured guests to come to table.

The Guests *rise hastily.*

What a gorgeous livery!

He has invited us!

I said there was some misunderstanding.

Man is so kind. Probably they are themselves not yet seated.

I asked whether there was not some one looking for us.

What a livery!

They say the dinner is magnificent.

Nothing can be bad in the house of Man.

What music! What an honour to be at the ball of Man!

Let those envy us who——

How gorgeous!

How sumptuous!

What an honour!

What an honour!

>*Repeating these words they withdraw one after another, and the hall becomes empty. The dancers, couple after couple, stop dancing, and without speaking walk out after the other guests. For some little time afterward one couple circle about, but they, too, soon follow the others. The musicians, however, continue to play with the same desperate painstaking.*
>
>*A lackey extinguishes the chandeliers, leaving only one light in the farthest chandelier, and goes out. In the dimness that ensues, the figures of the musicians can be seen as vague, wavering forms, their bodies rocking with their instruments. The* Being in Grey *stands out sharply. The flame of the candle flickers and illuminates his stony face and chin with a bright, yellowish light.*

Without raising his head, he turns and, illuminated by the flame of the candle, walks with calm and silent footsteps across the hall to the door through which MAN *passed, and disappears through it.*

Curtain.

ACT IV

MISFORTUNE

A large, rectangular room of a gloomy aspect. The walls, ceiling, and floor are smooth and dark. In the rear wall are two tall, eight-paned, curtainless windows, between which is a low door. Two similar windows are in the right wall. Night is looking in at the windows, and when the door is open the same deep blackness peers quickly into the room. In general, however much light there may be in the rooms of MAN, *the large, dark, windows seem to devour it.*

The left wall is pierced by a single low door leading into the inner apartments. Against this wall stands a broad divan covered with dark cloth. At the window on the right is the work-table of MAN, *very plain and cheap. On it is a dimly burning lamp with a dark shade, under which a design spread out on the table makes a yellow square. On the table also are a child's toys—a little soldier cap, a wooden horse without a tail, and a red, long-nosed clown with bells. Against the wall between the windows is a shabby old bookcase, entirely empty. On the shelves can be seen streaks of dust, showing that the books have been recently removed. There is but one chair.*

In a corner darker than the other corners stands the BEING IN GREY, *called* HE. *The candle in his hand is no higher than it is broad. It is only a stub and is beginning to flatten out as it melts. It burns with a reddish, flickering light and casts red spots upon the* BEING'S *stony face and chin.*

THE LIFE OF MAN

MAN'S *only servant, an* OLD WOMAN, *is seated in the chair. She speaks in a monotonous voice, addressing an imaginary companion:*

MAN is poor again. He had many valuable things—horses, and carriages, and even an automobile—but everything is gone now, and of all his servants I alone am left. In this room and in two others there are still some fine things, like the divan there and the bookcase, but in the remaining twelve rooms there is nothing. They stand empty and dark. Day and night the rats run about in them and fight and shriek. People are afraid of the rats, but I am not. It's all the same to me.

For a long time an iron plate has been hanging at the carriage entrance with a notice that the house is for sale, but nobody buys. The plate is rusty and the letters on it are worn away by the rains, but no one comes and no one buys. No one has use for the old house. But perhaps some one will buy some day. Then we shall go and hunt for another place, and the new place will seem very strange. My mistress will begin to weep, and perhaps even the old gentleman will weep. But not I. It's all the same to me.

You wonder where the wealth has gone? I don't know. Perhaps you are surprised at that, but, you see, all my life I have worked in private families and I frequently have seen their money disappear quietly through some crevice or other. So it was with this family. At first there was much; then there was less; then nothing at all. Customers used to come and give orders, and then they stopped coming. Once I asked the lady why this was so, and she answered: "They cease to like what they used to like. They cease to love what they used to love." I asked: "How can it be that people cease to like a thing when once they have come to like it?" She did not answer and began to cry. But I didn't. It's all the same to me. It's all the same to me.

As long as they pay me, I will live with them. If they stop paying, I will go somewhere else and live with others. I have cooked for them; when I leave, I shall cook for others; and after a while, I'll stop entirely; for I shall be old and my eyesight poor. Then they will drive me away and say: "Go where you like. We will hire some one else." But what of that? I'll go. It's all the same to me.

People are surprised at me. They say it is frightful to live here; that it is frightful to sit evenings with only the wind whistling in the chimney and the rats shrieking and gnawing.

I don't know; perhaps it is frightful, only I don't think about it. Why should I? They sit quietly and look at each other and listen to the wind, and I sit by myself alone in the kitchen and also listen to the wind. Isn't it the same wind that whistles in our ears? Young people used to come and visit their son, and then they would all laugh and sing and go into the empty rooms and chase away the rats. But no one comes to me and I sit alone, all alone. There is no one to talk with, so I talk to myself. It's all the same to me.

And so they are in straits. Three days ago another misfortune came. The young gentleman went out for a walk. He put his hat on one side of his head and smoothed back his hair, as young men do. But a wicked man threw a stone at him from behind a corner and cracked his skull like a nut. They brought him home and laid him down, and he is lying there now, dying—or perhaps he will live. Who knows? The master and the mistress wept, and then they took all the books and loaded them on a dray and sold them; and now they have hired a nurse with the money and bought medicine. They even bought some grapes. So the books were of some use after all. However, he can't eat the grapes. He can't even look at them. So they lie there by him on a plate—just lie there.

  Doctor *enters by the outside door. He is gloomy and much worried.*

Doctor. Am I in the right house? Do you know, old lady? I am the doctor. I make many calls and often I go to the wrong place. They call me here, they call me there; but all the houses look alike and the people are tiresome in all of them. Is this the right place?

Old Woman. I don't know.

Doctor. Just let me look in my note-book. Is there a child here with sore throat—choking?

Old Woman. No.

Doctor. Young man choking on a bone?

Old Woman. No.

Doctor. Man here who suddenly went crazy from poverty and killed his wife and two children with an axe? There ought to be four in all.

Old Woman. No.

Doctor. Young girl whose heart has stopped beating? Don't lie to me, old woman. I think she is here.

Old Woman. No.

Doctor. No? I believe you. You seem to speak sincerely. Have you a young man whose skull was broken with a stone and who is dying?

Old Woman. Yes. Go through that door at the left into the next room; but don't go farther, or the rats will eat you.

Doctor. Very well. They're always ringing my door-bell, day and night. See, it's night now. The street lights are all put out, but I am still on the go. I often make mistakes, old woman.

  He goes out through the door which leads to the inner part of the house.

OLD WOMAN. One doctor attended him but didn't cure him, and now there is another, and probably he won't cure him, either. But what's the odds? Their son will die and we shall be left alone in the house. I shall sit in the kitchen and talk to myself, and they will sit in this room in silence, thinking, and there will be one more room for the rats to run and fight in. Let them run and fight. It's all the same to me. It's all the same to me.

You ask me why the wicked man hit the young master? I don't know. How should I know why people kill one another? One threw a stone from behind a corner and ran away, and the other fell down, and now he is dying. That's all I know. They say that our young master was kind and brave and always took the part of the wretched. I don't know. It's all the same to me. Good or bad, young or old, alive or dead, it's all the same to me. It's all the same to me.

As long as they pay me, I'll stay. If they stop paying, I'll go somewhere else and cook for others; and after a while I'll stop entirely; for I shall be old, and my eyesight poor, and I shan't be able to tell salt from sugar. Then they will drive me away, and say: "Go where you like. We will hire some one else." But what of that? I'll go. It's all the same to me. Here or there or nowhere—it's all the same to me, all the same to me.

> *Enter* DOCTOR, MAN, *and his* WIFE. MAN *and his* WIFE *have perceptibly aged, and are entirely grey.* MAN'S *long hair, rising high above his head, and his large beard make his head resemble that of a lion. Though he walks slightly bent, he holds his head erect and looks out sternly and resolutely from beneath his grey brows. When he looks at anything near, he puts on large spectacles with silver rims.*

DOCTOR. Your son has fallen into a sound sleep. Don't

wake him up. Perhaps the sleep will do him good. You go to sleep, too. If a man has time to sleep, he ought to sleep, and not to walk about and talk.

WIFE. Thank you, doctor. You have so reassured us. Will you not come again to-morrow?

DOCTOR. I will come to-morrow and the day after to-morrow. You go to sleep, too, old woman. It's already night and time for every one to sleep. Do I go through this door? I frequently make mistakes.

He goes out. The OLD WOMAN *also goes out.* MAN *and his* WIFE *remain.*

MAN. See, Wife, here is a design I began before our son was hurt. When I had drawn this line I stopped and said to myself: "After I have rested a little I will go to work again." How simple a line it is; how quiet and yet how frightful! Perhaps it is the last that I shall draw while our son is alive. How calm, how simple it is, and yet how full of foreboding!

WIFE. Don't worry, my dear. Dismiss these apprehensions. I believe that the doctor told the truth and that our son will recover.

MAN. But are you not worried? Look at yourself in the mirror. You are as white as your hair, my dear companion.

WIFE. Of course I am a little anxious; still I am sure there is no danger.

MAN. My poor armour-bearer! Steadfast guardian of my blunted sword! Now, as always, you beguile and cheer me by your sincerity and devotion. Your old knight is now broken and his withered hand cannot long hold his weapon. But what is this? Our son's toys! Who put them here?

WIFE. My dear, you forget. You put them here yourself some time ago. You said then that you could work better with these simple child's toys lying before you.

MAN. Oh, yes; I had forgotten. But now they are like

instruments of torture and execution to a man condemned to death. When a child dies, his toys become a curse to the living. Oh, Wife, Wife! The very sight of them is terrible!

WIFE. We bought them when we were poor. It saddens me to look at them. Poor, dear toys!

MAN. I cannot bear it. I must take them in my hands. See, here is the horse with the broken tail. "Gid-ap, gid-ap, horsie! Where are you galloping?" "Far, papa, far away into the fields and the green woods." "Take me with you, horsie." "Gid-ap, gid-ap! Climb on, dear papa—" And here's the soldier's cap made of pasteboard. Poor little cap, which I myself tried on laughingly when I bought it in the shop: "Who are you?" "I am a knight, papa. I am the strongest, bravest knight that ever was." "Where are you going, my little knight?" "I am going to kill the dragon, dear papa. I am going to free the captives, papa." "Ride on, ride on, my little knight!" [*The* WIFE *of* MAN *weeps*] And see, here is our clown, just as he always looked, with his dear, stupid grin. He is as tattered as if he had been through a hundred fights, but he is still laughing and his nose is as red as ever. Come, ring your bells, my friend, as you used to ring them. You can't? Only one bell left, you say? Well, then, I'll throw you on the floor. [*He throws the toy down.*

WIFE. What are you doing? Remember how often our child has kissed his funny little face.

MAN. Yes, I was wrong. Forgive me, my dear, and you, little toy, forgive me, too. [*He picks up the toy, bending his knees with difficulty*] Still smiling! Come, I will lay you a little farther away. Don't be angry; I cannot look at your smile just now. Go and smile somewhere else.

WIFE. Your words wring my heart. Believe me, our son will recover. Would it be just for the young to die before the old?

MAN. Where have you ever seen justice in this world, Wife?

WIFE. My beloved, I beg you, kneel with me in prayer to God.

MAN. It is hard for my old knees to bend.

WIFE. Bend them—it is your duty.

MAN. God will not hear me, for never yet have I troubled his ear either with praise or with petition. Do you pray; you are the mother.

WIFE. No, you must pray; you are the father. If a father doesn't pray for his son, who will? To whose hands will you commit him? Could I speak alone as we two can speak together?

MAN. Let it be as you say. Perhaps, if I bend my aged knees, eternal justice will answer.

They both fall on their knees, their faces turned toward the corner where the UNKNOWN *stands motionless, and their hands folded on their breasts in attitude of prayer.*

PRAYER OF THE MOTHER

O God, I beseech you, let my son live. That is all I know, that is all I can say—only this one thing: "God, let my son live." I cannot frame other words. All about me is dark. All is falling away. I understand nothing, and my soul is so filled with horror, O Lord, that I can say only one thing. O God, let my son live, let my son live! Let him live! Forgive me for uttering so poor a prayer, but I cannot do otherwise, O Lord; you know I cannot. Look upon me, only look upon me. Do you see, do you see how my head trembles? Do you see how my hands shake? And what are my hands, O Lord? Have mercy upon him! He is so young. He has a birthmark on his right arm. Let him live, if only a little while, only a little while! He is only a child, and so innocent. He still loves sweets, and I bought him some grapes. Have mercy, have mercy!

She weeps silently, covering her face with her hands. Without looking at her MAN *speaks.*

PRAYER OF THE FATHER

See, I am praying to you. I have bent my aged knees. I have fallen in the dust before you. See, I kiss the earth. Perhaps I have sometimes offended you. In that case, pardon me, pardon me. It is true that I have been presumptuous and overbold, that I have demanded instead of beseeching, and that I have often reproached you for your acts. Pardon me. If you desire, if such is your will, punish me. Only spare my son; spare him, I pray you. I do not beg for mercy or for pity; no, I beg only for justice. You are old and I, too, as you see, am old. You will understand my prayer the better for that. Wicked people tried to kill him, people who by their evil deeds insult you and pollute the earth—malicious, brutal, villainous people, who throw stones from behind corners—from behind corners, the villains! Let not this wicked thing be done. Stanch his blood. Bring back his life, bring back life to my fine boy. You have taken everything from me, but have I ever importuned you? Have I said, Restore my wealth, restore my friends, restore my genius? No, never. I never asked you even for my genius, and you know what genius means—how it is more to one than life itself. It is the will of fate, I thought, and I bore everything, I bore everything, I bore it proudly. But now, on my knees in the dust, kissing the earth, I beg of you, bring back life to my son. I kiss the earth.

They rise. The BEING *called* HE *listens with indifference to the prayer of the father and the mother.*

WIFE. I fear that your prayer, my dear, was not sufficiently humble. There seemed to be a note of pride in it.

MAN. No, no, Wife. I said what was right, just as a man should speak. Should He love cringing flatterers more than bold, proud people who speak the truth? No, Wife, you don't understand. Now I have faith, now I am calm, even cheerful. I feel that I am still of some service to my son, and that heartens me. See whether he is sleeping. He ought to be sleeping soundly.

> *The* WIFE *goes out.* MAN *casts a friendly glance into the corner where the* BEING IN GREY *stands. He takes up the toy clown, plays with it, and gently kisses its long, red nose. At this moment the* WIFE *comes in and* MAN, *somewhat embarrassed, says:* "I offended this poor fool, but now I have begged pardon for everything. Well, how is our dear son?"

WIFE. He is very pale.

MAN. That's nothing. It will pass. He has lost a great deal of blood.

WIFE. His pale, shaved head is so pitiful to see. He had such beautiful golden curls.

MAN. They cut them off in order to wash the wound. But never mind, Wife, never mind. They will grow out still finer. Did you gather them up? They must be gathered up and preserved. His precious blood is on them, Wife.

WIFE. Yes, I have laid them away in the jewel box, all that is left of our wealth.

MAN. Do not lament the loss of our wealth. Wait until our son begins to work. He will win back all that we have lost. Now I am cheerful, my dear, I have faith in our future. Do you remember our poor rose-tinted room? The good neighbours strewed oak leaves about it, and you made a wreath for my head and said I was a genius.

WIFE. And I say it even now, my dear. If other people have ceased to value you, I have not.

MAN. No, my dear little Wife, you are wrong. The creations of genius live longer than this wretched old garment that we call our body, but even during my lifetime my works are——

WIFE. No, they are not dead and will never die. Recall the house on the corner which you built ten years ago. Every evening at sunset you go to look at it. Is there in the whole city a building more beautiful, more meaningful?

MAN. True. I so built it that the last rays of the setting sun might fall upon it and set its windows ablaze. After the whole city is in darkness, my building is still bidding farewell to the sun. That was work well done, and perhaps it will outlive me, if only a little. Don't you think so?

WIFE. Of course it will, my dear.

MAN. One thing grieves me, Wife. Why am I so soon forgotten? I might have been remembered a little longer, my dear, a little longer.

WIFE. People forget what they once knew. They cease to love what they once loved.

MAN. They might have remembered me somewhat longer, somewhat longer.

WIFE. I saw a young artist near the house. He was studying the building carefully and was making a sketch of it in his note-book.

MAN. Why did you not tell me of that, my dear? That is significant, very significant. It means that my thoughts will pass on to others, and even though I am forgotten, yet my thoughts will live on. That is very important, extremely important.

WIFE. They have certainly not forgotten you, my dear.

Think of the young man who bowed to you so respectfully on the street.

MAN. True, Wife. A fine young man, very. He had a glorious young face. It is well that you remind me of this. It has filled my soul with sunshine. But I feel sleepy. I am probably tired. Yes; and I am old. My grey little Wife, do you see that I am old?

WIFE. You are still as handsome as ever.

MAN. And my eyes shine?

WIFE. Yes, your eyes shine.

MAN. And my hair is black as pitch?

WIFE. It is as white as snow, which is even more handsome.

MAN. And I have no wrinkles?

WIFE. There are a few little wrinkles, but——

MAN. Of course. I know that I am a handsome fellow. To-morrow I will buy a uniform and enter the light brigade. Won't that be fine?

WIFE. [*Smiling*] Now you are joking as you used. Well, lie down, my dear, and take a short nap and I will go to our son. Rest quietly; I will not leave him until he wakes, and then I will call you. You don't like to kiss my wrinkled old hand, do you? [MAN *kisses it.*

MAN. Nonsense! You are the most beautiful woman in the world.

WIFE. But the wrinkles?

MAN. Wrinkles? I see a dear, kind, good, intelligent face; nothing more. Don't be angry with me for my harshness. Go to our son. Guard him. Sit by him like a quiet shadow of tenderness and comfort. And if he grows restless in his sleep, sing him a little song as of old. And set the grapes nearer so that he can reach them.

The WIFE *goes out.* MAN *lies down on the lounge with his head toward the corner where the* BEING IN GREY *stands motionless.* MAN's *position is such that the hand of the* BEING *almost touches his grey, dishevelled hair. He quickly falls asleep.*

THE BEING IN GREY. Man, flattered by his hopes, has fallen into a deep and grateful sleep. His breathing is as quiet as a child's, and his aged heart, resting from its sufferings, beats calmly and evenly. He does not know that in a few moments his son will die. And, as he sleeps, in his mysterious fancies an impossible happiness rises before him.

He dreams that he is riding with his son in a white boat over a beautiful, smooth river. He dreams that it is a beautiful day and that he sees the blue sky and the transparent, crystal water. He hears the reeds rustle as they part before the boat. He is filled with joy and he fancies that he is blessed. All his emotions are deceiving him.

But suddenly he becomes restless. The terrible truth, penetrating the dense veil of his dreams, has seared his thought.

"Why is your golden hair cut so short, my boy; why is it?"

"My head ached, father, and that is why my hair was cut so short."

And again deceived, Man is happy and sees the blue sky and hears the reeds rustling as they part.

He does not know that his son is already dying. He does not hear how in a last wild hope, with childish faith in the power of older persons, his son calls him, without words, with the cry of his heart, "Papa, papa, I am dying! I am slipping away! Hold me!" Man's sleep is deep and joyous, and in his mysterious and deceiving visions an impossible happiness rises before him.

Awake, Man! Your son is dead!

ACT IV   THE LIFE OF MAN   127

MAN. [*Terrified, raises his head and gets up*] Ah! Did some one call me?

> *At the same moment the weeping of many women is heard in the next room. With high-pitched voices they are uttering long-drawn-out lamentation over the dead. Enter the* WIFE, *pale as death.*

MAN. Is our son dead?

WIFE. Yes, he is dead.

MAN. Did he call me?

WIFE. No, he did not wake. He called no one. He is dead, my son, my precious child!

> *She falls on her knees before* MAN *and sobs, throwing her arms about his knees.* MAN *places his hand upon her head, and, in a voice choked with sobs but threatening, he speaks, his face toward the corner where the* BEING IN GREY *stands, indifferent.*

MAN. You have offended a woman, villain! You have killed our boy. [*The* WIFE *sobs.* MAN *with trembling hand quietly smooths her hair*] Don't weep, my dear, don't weep. He will laugh at our tears, as he laughed at our prayers. But you (I know not who you are, God, the Devil, Fate, or Life)—I curse you.

> *He speaks the following with a loud, strong voice, with one hand held over his wife, as if to defend her, the other threateningly extended toward the* UNKNOWN.

THE CURSE OF MAN

I curse all that you have given me! I curse the day on which I was born! I curse the day on which I shall die! I curse my whole life, my joys, and my grief! I curse myself! I curse my eyes, my ears, my tongue! I curse my heart, my head! And I hurl all back into your cruel face, senseless Fate! Be accursed, be accursed for ever! Through my curse I rise victorious above you. What more can you do to me? Hurl me upon the ground, yes, hurl me down! I shall only laugh and cry out, "Be accursed!" Fetter my lips with the clamps of death, and my last thought shall be a cry into your ass's ears, "Be accursed, be accursed!" Seize upon my corpse, gnaw it like a dog, worry it in the darkness, —I am not within it. I have vanished and, vanishing, I repeat the curse, "Be accursed, be accursed!" Over the head of the woman whom you have offended, over the body of the boy whom you have killed, I hurl upon you the curse of Man!

He stands in silence with his hand raised in a threatening attitude. The BEING IN GREY *listens with indifference to the curse, and the flame of the candle flutters as if blown by the wind. For some time the two stand facing each other in a tense silence—*MAN *and the* BEING IN GREY. *The crying in the next room becomes louder and more prolonged and gradually passes into a rhythmical wailing.*

Curtain.

ACT V

THE DEATH OF MAN

A vague, wavering, flickering, dim light through which one can at first make out nothing. When the eye becomes accustomed to the gloom, the following scene is disclosed:

A long, wide, basement room with a very low ceiling and without windows. A flight of stairs leads from the room to the entrance, somewhere above. The walls are smooth, gloomy, and dirty, like the coarse, spotted hide of some huge beast. The rear wall, as far as to the steps, is occupied by a large, flat buffet with a mirror. The buffet is filled with straight rows of bottles containing liquids of various colours. Behind a low counter sits the BARTENDER, *perfectly motionless, with his hands folded across his stomach. He has a white face with red nose and cheeks, a bald head, and a large, sandy beard, and wears an expression of complete calm and indifference. He remains the same through the entire scene, not once moving from his place or changing his attitude. At small tables sit the* DRUNKARDS, *on wooden stools. The number of the people is seemingly increased by their shadows, which rove along the walls and ceiling.*

The scene presents an endless variety of the disgusting and the horrible. The faces resemble masks, the parts of which are disproportionately large or small. Some have large noses, others are entirely noseless. The eyes roll wildly, almost bursting from their sockets, or are nearly closed so that they are reduced to scarcely visible slits and points. There are prominent Adam's apples and diminutive chins. All have tangled, shaggy, and dirty hair, which in some cases half conceals the face. In spite of their variety, all the faces have a hideous resemblance, which consists in a sallow, grave-like colour and an expression now of frightful laughter and now of insane and gloomy horror.

The DRUNKARDS *are dressed in rags of one colour, which expose a sallow, bony hand, or a sharp knee, or a sunken, frightful chest. Some are nearly naked. The women are scarcely distinguishable from the men and are even uglier. The hands and heads of all tremble, and their gait is unsteady, as if they were walking on very slippery or boggy or moving surfaces. Their voices, too, are alike in that they are wheezing, whimpering, and as unsteady as the gait. They utter their words with lips which do not obey them and which are, as it were, stiffened with cold.*

In the centre of the group, at a separate table, sits MAN, *resting his grey, dishevelled head upon his hands. He remains throughout in the same position, except for the moment that he speaks. He is shabbily dressed.*

In one corner the BEING IN GREY *with the nearly burned-out candle stands motionless. The narrow, blue flame flutters, now bending to one side and now reaching upward with a sharp tongue, throwing livid spots of light on His stony face and chin.*

CONVERSATION OF THE DRUNKARDS

My God! My God!

Listen! How strangely everything shakes! You cannot fix your eyes on anything.

Everything trembles as in a fever: people, chairs, and the ceiling.

Everything sways as if it were afloat.

Don't you hear a noise? I hear a noise as if iron wheels were rumbling or stones were falling from a cliff—huge stones, falling like rain.

That is the noise in your ears.

That is the noise of the blood. I can feel my blood, thick, black, and smelling of rum. It rolls heavily along the veins, and when it comes to the heart everything seems to fall and terror seizes me.

I seem to see lightning flashes.

I see huge, red bonfires and people burning in them. There's a disgusting smell of burning flesh! Black shadows whirl about the bonfires, drunken shadows. Ho, there! Let me have a dance with you!

My God! My God!

I, too, am cheerful. Who will laugh with me? No one wants to. Then I will laugh alone. [*He laughs alone.*

A charming woman is kissing my lips. She smells of musk and her teeth are like a crocodile's. She is trying to bite me. Away, you slattern!

I am not a slattern. I am an old, pregnant serpent. For an hour I have been watching the little serpents issuing from my body and crawling about. Take care! Don't crush my little snakes!

Where are you going?

Who's walking about there? Sit down! The whole house shakes when you walk.

I can't sit still. It is frightful when I sit still.

It is frightful for me, too. When I sit still I can feel horror running through my body.

So can I. Let me go!

Three or four drunkards wander aimlessly about with unsteady steps, stumbling among the tables.

See what it is doing! For two hours it has been trying

to jump onto my knees. It comes within an inch of it. I drive it away, but it comes back. That's a queer sort of game.

Black cockroaches are creeping about under my skull, making a crawling noise.

My brain is falling to pieces. I can feel one grey fragment separate from the other. My brain is like spoiled cheese—it smells.

It smells like carrion here.

My God! My God!

To-night I will crawl to her on my knees and butcher her. Blood will flow. It is flowing now—red blood.

Three people are continually following me. They are calling me into a dark, lonely corner. They want to butcher me there. They are gathered about the door now.

Who is that walking along the walls and ceiling?

My God! They have come—they're after me!

Who?

They.

My tongue is numb. What shall I do? My tongue is numb. I will weep. [*He weeps.*

Everything in me is coming out. I shall turn inside out in a moment and be red.

Listen, listen! Ho, somebody! A monster is coming upon me. It is raising its hand. Help! Oh!

What's this? Help! A spider!

Help!

[*For some time they cry with hoarse voices:* "Help!"

We are all drunkards. Let's call everybody down here. Up yonder it is nasty.

No, don't. When I go out on the street, the street rushes about like a wild beast and quickly throws me to the ground.

We have all come here from the street. We drink alcohol and it makes us happy.

It makes us miserable. All day I tremble with horror.

Better this horror than life. Who wants to go back there?

Not I.

Nor I. I'd rather die here. I don't want to live.

Nobody wants to live.

My God! My God!

Why does Man come here? He drinks little and sits long. We do not need him.

Let him go home. He has a home.

He has fifteen rooms.

Don't touch him! He has nowhere else to go.

He has fifteen rooms.

But they are empty, except for the rats. The rats run about in them and fight.

But his wife?

He has nobody. Probably his wife is dead.

His wife is dead.

His wife is dead.

> *During this conversation and that which follows, the* Old Women *in strange garments enter noiselessly and without attracting attention replace the quietly withdrawing* Drunkards. *They mingle in the conversation, but so gradually that no one notices it.*

Conversation of the Drunkards and the Old Women

Old Woman. He will soon die. He is so feeble he can scarcely walk.

Drunkard. He has fifteen rooms.

Old Woman. Listen to his heart. How unevenly and feebly it beats. It will soon stop.

DRUNKARD. Invite us to your house, Man. You have fifteen rooms.

OLD WOMAN. It will soon stop—the big, old, feeble heart of Man.

DRUNKARD. He is asleep, the drunken fool. It is frightful to sleep, and yet he sleeps on. He might die in his sleep. Hey, there! Wake him up!

OLD WOMAN. Do you recall how his heart used to beat—fresh and strong?

Subdued laughter.

DRUNKARD. Who's laughing? There are intruders here.

DRUNKARD. Only in your imagination. There is no one here but us—us drunkards.

DRUNKARD. I will go out on the street and raise a disturbance. I have been robbed. I am completely naked. I have a green skin.

OLD WOMAN. Good evening.

DRUNKARD. Again the wheels are rumbling. My God! They will crush me. Help!

No one answers.

OLD WOMAN. Good evening.

OLD WOMAN. Do you remember how he was born?

OLD WOMAN. I think you were there.

DRUNKARD. It must be I am dying. My God! My God! Who will carry me to the grave? Who will bury me? I shall lie about like a dog in the street. People will walk over me. Carriages will ride over me. They will crush me. My God! My God! [*He weeps.*

OLD WOMAN. Allow me to congratulate you, my dear kinsman, on the birth of your son.

DRUNKARD. I am firmly convinced that there is an error here. A straight line that presents the form of a closed circle is simply ridiculous.

DRUNKARD. I will prove it to you in a jiffy.
DRUNKARD. You are quite right.
DRUNKARD. My God! My God!
DRUNKARD. Only people who are ignorant of mathematics will admit it. I won't admit it. Do you hear? I won't admit it.
OLD WOMAN. Do you remember the rose-coloured dress and the naked throat?
OLD WOMAN. And the flowers—the lilies-of-the-valley on which the dew had not yet dried, and the violets, and the green grass?
OLD WOMAN. Don't touch them, girls! Don't touch the flowers!

Subdued laughter.

DRUNKARD. My God! My God!

The DRUNKARDS are all gone. Their places are occupied by the OLD WOMEN with strange garments. The light, though very faint, becomes steady. The figure of the UNKNOWN comes sharply out as does also the grey head of MAN, upon which from above falls a feeble light.

CONVERSATION OF THE OLD WOMEN

Good evening.
Good evening. What a glorious night!
Well, we are together again. How are you?
I have a cough.

Subdued laughter.

It won't be long now. He will soon die.
Look at the candle. The flame is blue and narrow and droops toward the sides. There is no wax left now—only the wick is burning.
It does not want to go out.

When did you ever see a flame that wanted to go out?

Stop quarrelling! Stop quarrelling! Whether it wants to go out or not, time is passing.

Do you remember his automobile? Once it almost crushed me.

And his fifteen rooms?

I have just been there. I was nearly eaten by the rats, and I caught cold from the draughts. Now that some one has stolen the windows, the wind sweeps through the whole house.

Did you lie on the bed where his wife died? How soft it is, isn't it?

Yes, I went through all the rooms and mused a bit. They have such a dear nursery. Only it is too bad that the windows are broken there, too, and the wind rustles amid the dust. The child's little bed is so dear! The mice have now built their nests in it and are raising their families.

Such dear little naked micelets.

Subdued laughter.

And in the study on the table lie the toys—the horse without a tail, the soldier cap, and the red-nosed clown. I played a bit with them. I put on the cap. It quite becomes me. But there's a terrible lot of dust on them. I was just covered with dirt.

But were you not in the hall where the dance took place? It is so cheerful there!

Yes, I was there, but just imagine what I saw. It was dark. The panes were all broken and the wind was rustling in the wall-paper——

It makes a sound like music.

And along the wall in the darkness were squatted the guests. Oh, if you only knew how they looked!

We know!
And with grinning teeth they barked abruptly: "How costly! How gorgeous!"
Surely you are joking!
Of course I am joking. You know how jolly I am.
How costly! How luxurious!
How gorgeous!

> *Subdued laughter.*

Remind him.
How costly! How gorgeous!
Do you remember the music at your ball?
He will soon die.
The dancers circled about and the music played so tenderly, so beautifully. This is the way it played.

> *They form a semicircle about* MAN *and in a low voice hum the tune that was played at the ball.*

Let's have a ball. It is so long since I have danced.
Just imagine that this is a palace, a miraculously beautiful palace.
Call the musicians! You cannot have a good dance without music.
Musicians!
Do you remember?

> *They strike up the tune and at the same moment the three musicians who played at the ball descend the stairs. The one with a violin carefully spreads the handkerchief over his shoulder, and all three begin to play with extreme painstaking, though the sounds are low, soft, and sad as in a dream.*

Now we have a ball!
How costly! How gorgeous!
How brilliant!

Do you remember?

Humming in a low tone in time with the music, they begin to circle about MAN, *posturing and repeating with wild distortions the movements of the girls in white robes who danced at the ball. During the first musical phrase they circle about, and during the second they approach each other and then draw apart gracefully and silently. They whisper in low voices.*

Do you remember?

You will soon die, but do you remember?

Do you remember?

Do you remember?

You will soon die, but do you remember?

Do you remember?

The dance becomes swifter and the movements more jerky. Through the voices of the OLD WOMEN *who are singing there glide strange, whimpering notes; and the same strange laughter, as yet subdued, runs like a low rustling through the dancers. As they sweep past* MAN *they discharge, as it were, into his ears abrupt whispers:*

Do you remember?

Do you remember?

How tender! How fine!

How restful to the soul!

Do you remember?

You will soon die. You will soon die. You will soon die——

Do you remember?

The whirling dance becomes swifter and the movements still more abrupt. Suddenly all is silent and motionless. The musicians become rigid, with their instruments in their hands. The dancing women are motion-

less in the same attitudes in which the oncoming of silence found them.

MAN rises, straightens himself, throws back threateningly his beautiful grey head, and cries out in a challenging voice, unexpectedly loud and full of sorrow and anger. After each brief utterance there is a short but profound silence.

MAN. Where is my armour-bearer? Where my sword? Where is my shield? I am weaponless. Come hither quickly, quickly. Be accurs——

[He sinks upon a chair with head thrown back and dies. At the same instant the candle, flaring up, goes out, and a deep gloom envelops all objects. It is as though the gloom were pouring down the stairway and gradually spreading over everything. Only the face of MAN is illuminated. Low, indistinct conversation of the OLD WOMEN, whispering and interchanging laughter.

THE BEING IN GREY. Silence! Man is dead.

Profound silence, during which the same cold, indifferent voice repeats the words from the far distance like an echo: "Silence! Man is dead." Profound silence. Slowly the gloom becomes thicker, but the mice-like figures of the OLD WOMEN watchers can still be seen. Now quietly and silently they begin to circle about the corpse. Then they begin to hum in a low tone, and the musicians begin to play. The gloom becomes still more dense, and as the music and singing become louder and louder the wild dance becomes more unrestrained. They are no longer dancing but wildly whirling about the corpse, stamping and shrieking with continuous, wild laughter. Absolute darkness ensues. The face of the dead is still illumined, but presently that also vanishes. Black, impenetrable darkness.

In the darkness one can hear the movements of the wild dancers, the shrieking, the laughter, and the discordant and desperately loud sounds of the orchestra. Having attained their greatest intensity, all these sounds quickly withdraw somewhere and die away. Silence.

Curtain.

ACT V

THE DEATH OF MAN

(VARIANT)

[It was only after "The Life of Man" had been presented on the stage that I became convinced I had fallen into error —both as regards the form and also as regards the fundamental meaning of the play.

As for the form, I could be content to leave the play unchanged. Written in a period of doubts and fears, it might be allowed to stand as my first attempt at a neo-realistic drama. Sins against the fundamental meaning are, however, quite another matter.

Leaving it to others to judge how far I am right and how far I am wrong in my interpretation of the meaning of human life, I am bound, both for my own sake and for the purpose of greater consistency and clearness, to correct such defects in the play as either obscure its fundamental idea or present that idea in an incomplete and unfinished form.

In the fifth act, a variant of which I now offer, the most essential defect was the incorporation into the drama of a relatively incidental element, namely, the Drunkards, and the absence of so essential a group, and a group so important in life as the Heirs, who naturally complete the groups of Kinsmen, Friends, and Enemies of Man.

By introducing into the drama the barroom and the Drunkards I did not, of course, intend to imply that every man dies inevitably in a barroom. Nevertheless, several of my critics quite erroneously drew the following series of inferences: "I do not go to barrooms, consequently this is not true, consequently I shall never die, consequently what sort of a Life of Man is this?" But the loneliness of Man dying in misfortune, to suggest which these people, themselves so solitary and unfortunate, were introduced, may be indicated fully by the presence of the heirs. While the Drunkards merely give Man an opportunity to die in solitude, the Heirs, on the other hand, with the natural pitilessness of all successors, not only urge him to die, but actually force death upon him. *Succession* is an important element which I left out of consideration in my first picture of "The Death of Man."

Mercy was absent from my play, and this also seemed to many to be unjust. In the present version it is represented in the character of the Sister of Mercy, and although during the whole of the act she does not open her eyes once, yet her very presence bears witness to the fact that mercy really exists.

Reminding my readers, however, that justice is merely a new or as yet unexposed error, I bring to a close my explanations (perhaps superfluous) and submit this new version of "The Death of Man" to the kindly judgment of the reader.

AUTHOR.]

The high, gloomy room in which the SON *and the* WIFE *of* MAN *died. On everything lies the stamp of ruin and death. The walls are warped and threaten to fall. The corners are overspread with cobwebs—regular, light-coloured circles inextricably interlaced. From the sagging ceiling likewise hang dark-grey clumps of abandoned spider-webs. The two tall windows have been forced inward and are bent as though by the steady and persistent pressure of the infinitude of darkness which surrounds the house of* MAN. *Should* the windows not hold firm—should they fall inward—the darkness would pour into the room and extinguish the feeble, dying light by which it is illuminated.

In the rear wall a zigzag stairway leads upward to the rooms where once the ball was given. At the foot of the stairs the warped, decayed steps can be seen, but farther upward they are lost in a dense and frowning darkness. By this wall stands a bed under a sagging, torn baldachin—the bed on which the WIFE of MAN died.

On the right is the dark opening of a large, cold, long-disused fireplace, in which, in a great heap of grey, dead ashes, can be seen a white sheet of partly burned paper, apparently a design. Before the fireplace in an armchair MAN sits motionless, dying. In his torn gown and unkempt grey hair and beard one can see the complete abandonment and solitude of death. Some little distance from MAN, in an armchair of the same sort, sits a SISTER OF MERCY, fast asleep, a white cross on her breast. During the whole act she does not once waken.

About the dying man are seated the HEIRS, surrounding him closely in a circle of eagerly outstretched faces. There are seven of them, three women and four men. Their necks are greedily stretched out toward MAN, their mouths are half-opened, expressing avarice, and the fingers on their uplifted hands are hooked stiffly like the claws of birds of prey. Among them there are large, well-fed people, particularly one gentleman, whose fat body welters formlessly upon the chair; but, from the manner in which they sit and in which they look at MAN, one can see that they have been hungry all their lives, that all their lives they have been awaiting the inheritance, and that apparently they are still hungry.

In one corner the BEING IN GREY, with the candle nearly burned out, stands motionless. The narrow, blue flame flutters, *now bending to one side and now reaching upward with a sharp tongue, and throws livid spots of light on His stony face and chin.*

Conversation of the Heirs

They speak in loud voices.

Dear kinsman, are you sleeping?
Dear kinsman, are you sleeping?
Dear kinsman, are you sleeping or not? Answer us.
We are your friends.
Your heirs.
Answer us.

Man is silent. The Heirs change their voices to a loud whisper.

He says nothing.
He doesn't hear. He is deaf.
No, he is only pretending. He hates us, and he would be glad to drive us away, but he can't. We are his heirs.
Every time we come he looks at us as if we had come to kill him. As if he were not dying of himself!
The fool!
That's from old age. All people become fools in their old age.
No, it's his greed. He would be glad to carry everything with him to the grave. He doesn't know that man goes to the grave empty-handed.
Why do you so hate our dear kinsman?
Because he is slow in dying. [*Louder*] Old man, why don't you die? You are spoiling our life. You are robbing us. Your clothes are torn and rotten, your house is tumbling down, your furniture is getting old and losing its value.
That is true, he is robbing us.
Sh! Why shout?

Old man, you are stripping us of our own.
But perhaps our dear kinsman hears us.
Let him hear. It is always good to hear the truth.
But perhaps he has still enough strength to make a will and deprive us of the inheritance.
Do you think so?

> *They laugh affectedly. They speak softly with assumed tenderness, but yet so loud that* MAN *can hear them.*

Nonsense. He was always an intelligent man with a sense of humour, and he understands a joke perfectly well. Is it not true, my dear kinsman?
Of course we were joking.
We can wait any length of time; it is only that we are sorry for him. It's so sad to sit day and night all alone before the empty fireplace. Is it not true, dear kinsman?
Why doesn't he go to bed?
Oh, it is just a little whim. His wife died on this bed, and he will never allow any one to touch either the linen or the pillows.
But time has already touched them.
They smell of decay.
Everything here smells of decay. [*He sniffs.*
Really, when you stop to reflect that in this fireplace he used to burn whole logs so wastefully——
Do you remember his ball? Our dear kinsman scattered his money so freely.
Our money.
But do you remember how he petted his wife, that insignificant creature!
You had better add, "who deceived him."
Sh!
Who had a dozen paramours.
Sh! Sh!

Who lived with a lackey, yes, with her own lackey. I myself once saw them making eyes at each other.

However, she is dead. Don't slander the dead.

But it is so. I heard about it, too.

Poor deceived fool!

Do you see any adornments in his honoured grey hair?

Sh! Sh!

> *With exclamations of* "Silence!" "Silence!" *they interchange glances and laugh slyly.*

Man has no right to think only of himself. Considering how much he might have left and how little remains——

A mere pittance.

We must thank Providence even for what is left. Our honoured kinsman is so careless.

Just look at his gown. Isn't it shameful to treat an expensive garment so?

Is it really so expensive? I cannot see from here what kind of cloth it is.

Approach him cautiously and feel of it. It is silk.

> *One of the women goes up to dying* MAN *and, pretending that she is straightening his pillow, feels of the cloth. All watch her with curiosity.*

Silk!

> *By various gestures, the* HEIRS *express their disgust.* MAN *for an instant rouses a little and feebly calls:* "Water!"

What does he say? Did he hear us? What does he want?

MAN. Water! In God's name, water!

> *He ceases speaking. Several of the* HEIRS, *frightened, look here and there for water but do not find any. Voices in a tone of irritation and alarm :*

Water!

He is asking for water.

Yes, give him some water.

There isn't any water.

> *They all turn toward the sleeping* SISTER OF MERCY *and cry out, putting their hands to their mouths in the fashion of a megaphone:*

Sister of Mercy!

Sister of Mercy!

Sister of Mercy!

We are speaking to you, Sister of Mercy! The sick man wants some water.

Shake her. What do they pay her for, if she sits there all the time asleep?

If you want a Sister of Mercy that won't sleep, you must pay more. Can't you understand?

She is very tired. The poor woman is overworked.

Let her sleep. It is a pity to disturb her when she is sleeping so soundly. Dear kinsman, can't you wait a bit? The Sister is very tired and is sleeping.

> MAN *does not answer, and they all sit down again on their chairs in a semicircle. The feeble light which illuminates the room slowly grows dimmer and darkness rises in the corners. The darkness comes on heavily from somewhere above, down the staircase. It spreads over the ceiling and clings sullenly to every hollow in the walls.*

He is quiet again. Poor man!

How dark it is! Do you not see how dark it is?

When I stop to think that he may sit thus before the fireplace for a long time yet—weeks, perhaps months—then I feel like seizing him by his thin neck and strangling him.

Begging your pardon, sir, although you appear to be very solicitous about the inheritance, I must remark that I don't know who you are.

Neither do I. Neither do I.

You are simply a nobody—a man from the street! What right have you to the inheritance?

I am just as much an heir as you are.

No, sir, you are a scoundrel.

No, it is you who are a scoundrel.

Sh! Sh!

Drive him out! Away with him!

You are all scoundrels.

Sh! You will wake him up.

> *Savagely showing their teeth, they threaten each other with clinched fists.*

Gentlemen, the light is going out. I can scarcely see your faces.

We must be going. Another day is wasted.

We must be going.

Well, I will remain. I am not going to leave. This is my house; mine, mine, mine!

The rats will eat you here.

[*In a fury*] This is my house; mine, mine, mine!

One seventh part, Mr. Heir-from-the-Street—at best one seventh part.

It is my house; mine!

Gentlemen, it is getting dark.

Good night, dear kinsman.

Good night, dear kinsman.

Good night, dear kinsman.

> *One after another they go out, bowing low to* MAN. *Some of them raise the limp hand of dying* MAN *as it lies on the arm of the chair and gently press it. The* HEIR-FROM-THE-STREET *is left alone. With a contemptuous glance at silent* MAN *and the* SISTER OF MERCY, *he*

swiftly and with an angry expression examines the room. He touches the walls, feels of the upholstering on the chairs, and estimates with his eye that which he cannot reach with his hand. He goes to the bed on which the WIFE *of* MAN *died and tests the firmness of the linen, but when the rotten cloth tears in his fingers, the* HEIR, *furiously stamping his foot, scatters the pillows and the sheets. Then he walks resolutely up to the dying* MAN *and takes a position behind his back.*

SPEECH OF THE HEIR

Listen, old Man. You ought to die. Why insult death by hanging back? Be off. Free living things from your dead hand. It lies on everything with leaden weight. Look! All things are waiting eagerly for your death: these falling walls, this spider-web and the spider imprisoned in its circles, this dark fireplace—it used to breathe upon you with its warmth, but now it is summoning your worn-out body to the chill of the grave. Begone! Where you are going you will meet those who loved you, both in youth and in old age, and those who were beloved by you.

Silence.

Don't you believe it?

[*He turns to the corner where the* BEING IN GREY *stands.*

Ho, you! Tell him that his loved ones will meet him there, his son with the crushed head and his wife who died of sickness and grief.

Silence.

You, too, are silent? And all is silent? So be it. But whatever may await you, begone from here. I, the living, drive you forth from life, and when you die I will bless you. I will lay wreaths upon your coffin, and on the spot where your body will decay I will erect a monument—if it is not too expensive. Begone!

> *Silence. The* HEIR *again walks up and down the room, but the melancholy of the place, the continually increasing darkness, and the heavy silence frighten him. He moves anxiously about, as if he had forgotten where the exit is, and speaks in a hoarse voice.*

Sister of Mercy, wake up! Sister! Where is the door—where is the door? Sister of Mercy!

> *Silence. In various places almost simultaneously the* OLD WOMEN *appear, and there follows a nimble, silent game very entertaining to the* OLD WOMEN. *They block the exit of the* HEIR; *they circle about the room and, thus noiselessly thrusting him hither and thither, finally let him pass through to the door. Raising his hands above his head with an expression of horror, the* HEIR *runs out. Subdued laughter on the part of the* OLD WOMEN.

CONVERSATION OF THE OLD WOMEN

Good evening.

Good evening. What a glorious night!

Well, we are together again. How are you?

I have a cough.

> *Subdued laughter.*

It won't be long now. He'll soon die.

Look at the candle. The flame is blue and narrow and drooping toward the sides. The wax is already consumed—only the wick is left, and that will soon burn out.

It does not want to go out.

Did you ever see a flame that wanted to go out?

Stop quarrelling! Stop quarrelling! Whether the flame wants to go out or not, time is passing.

Time is passing.

Time is passing.

Do you recall his birth? Allow me to congratulate you, my dear kinsman, on the birth of your son.

Do you remember the rose-coloured dress and the naked throat?

And the flowers—the lilies-of-the-valley, on which the dew had not yet dried, and the violets, and the green grass?

Don't touch them, girls. Don't touch the flowers!

They laugh.

Time is passing.

Time is passing.

Laughter. One of the OLD WOMEN *puts the bed in order.*

What are you doing?

I am making the bed on which his wife died.

What's the use of that? He'll soon be dead.

Don't bother me. I am making the bed on which his wife died.

How kind you are!

Now all is right. Now he can go.

When He permits him.

Now all is right; now all is right.

Like a deep sigh there sweeps through the room a harmonious but very sad and strange sound. Originating somewhere above, it tremulously dies out in the dark corners. It is as though many harp-strings were snapping one after another.

Sh! Do you hear it?

What's that?

It's up above where the ball was. That's the music.

No, it's the wind. I was there; I saw it, and I know it is

the wind. The window-glass is broken and the wind is playing a chord over the sharp points of the glass.

It *is* like music.

How cheerful it is up there! The guests are squatting in the darkness by the tattered walls. Oh, if you only knew how they look!

We know.

And with grinning teeth they bark abruptly: "How costly!" "How gorgeous!"

Surely you are joking!

Of course I am joking. You know how jolly I am.

How costly! How gorgeous!

How brilliant!

> *Subdued laughter.*

Remind him.

> *They surround* MAN, *pressing close to him with gentle, caressing movements. They fondle him with their bony hands. They peer into his face and whisper slyly, probing the inmost recesses of his old heart.*

Do you remember?

How costly! How gorgeous!

Do you remember the music at your ball?

He will soon die.

The dancers circled about and the music played so tenderly, so beautifully. This is the way it went.

> *With low voices they hum the air of the music which was played at the ball.*

Do you remember?

Let's have a ball. It is so long since I have danced. Just imagine that this is a palace, a miraculously beautiful palace!

Do you remember? Hark, the singing violins pour forth

their notes! Hear how tenderly the flute sings! Hear how——

> *Strains of music, suddenly interrupting the speech of the* OLD WOMAN, *begin to play in the room above, where the ball was held. The sounds are loud and distinct. The* OLD WOMEN *listen attentively.*

Sh! Do you hear?

They are playing.

The musicians are playing.

> *One of them cries out in a loud voice:* "Ho, musicians! Hither!"
>
> *The others echo her:* "Ho, musicians! Hither! Ho, musicians! Hither!"
>
> *The music above ceases, and almost at the same moment the three musicians who played at the ball, issuing from the darkness, descend the warped staircase. They come out to the centre of the stage and stand in a row, as they stood before. The one with the violin carefully spreads a handkerchief over his shoulder, and all three begin to play with extreme painstaking. The sounds, however, are tender, low, and sad, as in a dream.*

Now we have a ball! How costly! How gorgeous! How brilliant!

Do you remember?

> *Humming softly in time to the music, they begin to circle about* MAN, *posturing and repeating with wild distortions the movements of the girls in white robes who danced at the ball. During the first musical phrase they circle about; during the second they approach each other and then draw apart gracefully and silently. They speak in loud whispers:*

Do you remember?

You will soon die, but do you remember?

Do you remember?
Do you remember?
You will soon die, but do you remember?
Do you remember?

> *The dance becomes swifter and the movements more jerky. Through the voices of the* OLD WOMEN *who are singing there glides a strange, whimpering note; and the same strange laughter, as yet subdued, runs through the dancers like a low rustling. As they sweep past* MAN *they discharge, as it were, into his ears abrupt whispers:*

Do you remember?
Do you remember?
How tender! How fine!
How restful to the soul!
Do you remember?
You will soon die! You will soon die! You will soon die——
Do you remember?

> *The whirling dance becomes swifter and the movements still more jerky. Suddenly all is silent and motionless. The musicians are petrified with their instruments in their hands; the dancing women stand motionless in the attitudes in which the oncoming of silence found them.*
>
> MAN *rises. With staggering, unsteady steps he walks toward the bed. One of the* OLD WOMEN *bars his way and whispers in his face:*

Don't lie on the bed; you will die there!
You will die there!
Beware of the bed!

> MAN *pauses, helpless, and sadly begs:* "Help me, somebody! I cannot reach the bed." *Suddenly the scales fall from his eyes. He sees the malicious*

OLD WOMEN *watching and mischievously sporting with death. He sees the ruin and darkness and destruction that pervade everything about him. He sees as if for the first time the stony face of the* BEING IN GREY *and the candle slowly burning out. He raises his hand and the* OLD WOMEN *give way before him. He throws back threateningly his grey-haired, beautiful head, stands erect, and, preparing for his last battle, he cries out in a challenging voice, unexpectedly loud and full of grief and anger. In the first brief expression one can still hear the feebleness of age, but with each succeeding utterance the voice becomes more youthful and stronger, and the candle, reflecting for a moment the life that has returned, flames up high, red and quavering, illuminating all about it with the sombre glow of a conflagration.*

MAN. Where is my armour-bearer? Where is my sword? Where is my shield? I am weaponless! Come quickly, quickly! Be accursed!

He falls at the foot of the bed and dies. At the same instant the flame of the candle with one last feeble flare goes out, and deep gloom envelops all objects. It is as if the walls and the windows that had formerly held back the darkness had finally given way and the darkness had flooded everything with a dense, black, triumphant wave. Only the face of MAN *is illumined. Low, indistinct conversation of the* OLD WOMEN *is heard, together with whispering and interchanging of laughter.*

BEING IN GREY. Silence! Man is dead.

Profound silence. The same cold, indifferent voice repeats the words from the far distance like an echo: "Silence! Man is dead." *Profound silence. Slowly the gloom becomes denser, though the mice-like figures of the* OLD WOMEN *watchers can still be seen. Quietly and silently they begin to circle about the corpse. Then they begin to hum in a low tone, and the musicians start playing. The gloom becomes still more dense, the music and singing louder and louder, and the wild dance more unrestrained. They are no longer dancing but wildly whirling about the corpse with stamping and shrieking and wild, uninterrupted laughter. Complete darkness ensues. The face of the dead is still illumined, but presently that also vanishes. Black, impenetrable darkness.*

In the darkness one can hear the movements of the wild dancers, the shrieking and laughter, and the discordant and desperately loud sounds of the orchestra. On attaining their highest pitch, all these sounds swiftly recede somewhere and die away. Silence.

Curtain.

THE SABINE WOMEN
A BIT OF ROMAN HISTORY
IN THREE ACTS

THE SABINE WOMEN
ACT I

A wild, rugged spot, at daybreak. As the sun rises, armed ROMANS *enter from the hills, dragging with them the beautiful but dishevelled* SABINE WOMEN. *The latter resist, scream, and scratch—all but one, who, perfectly quiet, seems to have fallen asleep in the arms of the* ROMAN *who carries her. The captors, groaning with the pain of their scratches, quickly drop the* WOMEN *in a heap and, hastily retreating, rearrange their clothing. They pant as if exhausted. The screaming subsides. The* WOMEN, *watching suspiciously the movements of the men, also set themselves to rights. They whisper and chatter in low tones.*

FIRST ROMAN. By Hercules! I'm as wet as a muskrat. I'll wager my woman weighed four hundred pounds at least.

SECOND ROMAN. You needn't have picked the biggest of the lot. For my part, I chose a thin little thing, and——

FIRST ROMAN. What's happened to your face? You don't mean to say that thin little thing——

SECOND ROMAN. Wow! She scratches like a cat.

FIRST ROMAN. They all scratch like cats. I have been in a hundred battles. I have been hacked with swords, beaten with clubs, bruised with stones. Gates and walls have fallen on me, but this is the worst yet. My Roman nose is a wreck.

THIRD ROMAN. If I hadn't been clean shaved in the ancient

Roman fashion, there wouldn't be a hair left on my face. You know what nice, slender fingers and what amazingly sharp nails they have. Well, talk about cats! Cats is no name for them. Mine never said a word, but all the way she just plucked out the down.

A TALL, FAT ROMAN. [*Speaks in a bass voice*] Mine got her hands under my breastplate and tickled me in the armpits so that I laughed the whole way.

A low, contemptuous laugh from the WOMEN.

FIRST ROMAN. Sh! They can hear us.

SECOND ROMAN. Come, gentlemen; stop your whining and spruce up. It would be a pity for the ladies to lose their respect for us on this very first day. Just look at Emilius Paulus. There's a man who keeps up his dignity.

THIRD ROMAN. Radiant as Aurora!

FOURTH ROMAN. By Hercules! Not a scratch on him. How did you manage it, Paulus?

PAULUS. [*With feigned modesty*] Oh, I don't know. She clung to me from the start as if I were her husband. You astonish me, gentlemen. Why, it was simplicity itself. When I took her up she spontaneously threw her arms about my neck. The only danger was that she would hug me to death. Her arms may be slender, but they are strong.

FIRST ROMAN. There's luck for you.

PAULUS. Simplicity itself, I tell you. Her innocent, confiding little heart told her that I loved her truly and respected her. Half the way she slept like a weary child, though you, of course, won't believe that.

THE FAT ROMAN. Pardon me, gentlemen, but how are we going to tell which is which? Having stolen them in the dark like chickens from a hen-coop——

From the group of WOMEN *comes the indignant exclamation:* "What a disgusting comparison!"

FIRST ROMAN. Sh! They can hear us.

THE FAT ROMAN. [*Lowering his voice an octave*] Well, how are we to pick them out? Mine was a very jolly sort, and I shan't give her up to anybody. And, anyway, I'm not going to let people tread on my toes.

SECOND ROMAN. Chucklehead!

THIRD ROMAN. I shall know mine by her voice. I shan't forget her screaming, come Christmas.

FOURTH ROMAN. I shall know mine by her nails.

SCIPIO. And I shall know mine by the wonderful fragrance of her hair.

PAULUS. And I mine by the modesty and beauty of her soul. O Romans! We stand on the threshold of a new life. Tedious solitude, farewell! Farewell, interminable nights, with your accursed nightingales! Let the nightingale sing now, or any other bird—I'm ready.

THE FAT ROMAN. Yes, it is time that we entered on the domestic stage of life.

> *Ironical exclamations from the* WOMEN: "Oh, yes! Why don't you try it? Come on!"

FIRST ROMAN. Sh! They can hear us.

SECOND ROMAN. It's high time—high time, I say.

THIRD ROMAN. Gentlemen, who goes first?

> *Silence. All stand motionless. Low, mocking laughter on the part of the* WOMEN.

THE FAT ROMAN. For my part, I've had all the tickling I want. Let some one else try it. And, anyway, I'm not going to let any one tread on my toes. Here, Paulus, you go.

PAULUS. Brute! Don't you see that my darling is still asleep? Look—that dark clump there under the stones—that's she. O innocent soul!

SCIPIO. Gentlemen, it is apparent from your attitude of indecision and from your confusion—a wholly justified confusion, I may say—that no one of you has the courage to approach these merciless creatures. Now, here is my plan——

THE FAT ROMAN. Wise head!

SCIPIO. Here, I say, is my plan. Let us advance in a body, and quite leisurely, each one hiding himself behind the others. Certainly, if we were not afraid of their husbands——

THE FAT ROMAN. Their husbands! Bosh!

Deep sighs from the WOMEN *and demonstrative weeping.*

FIRST ROMAN. Sh! They can hear us.

SCIPIO. There you go again, Mark Antony, with that mouth of yours. We must avoid this unlucky word husband. You see how it works on the feelings of these poor women. Well, gentlemen, do you agree to my plan?

THE ROMANS. Agreed! Agreed!

SCIPIO. Well, then, gentlemen——

The ROMANS *prepare for the attack, the* WOMEN *prepare to defend themselves. In the place of lovely faces are seen sharp finger-nails, ready to bury themselves in face and hair. A low, hissing is heard, as of snakes. The* ROMANS *advance in accordance with their plan; that is, each one hides himself behind some one else, with the result that they all fall back and take shelter in the wings. The* WOMEN *laugh. The* ROMANS *return to their places in confusion.*

FIRST ROMAN. It looks as if there were some flaw in your plan, Scipio. As Socrates would say, we advanced backward.

THE FAT ROMAN. I can't make head or tail of it.

PAULUS. Courage, gentlemen. What is a scratch or two? Once we have reached the goal, oh, what bliss! Forward, Romans! To the attack!

The ROMANS, *with the exception of* PAULUS, *who gazes dreamily at the heavens, rush upon the* WOMEN *in a*

THE SABINE WOMEN

disorderly crowd, but, after a moment of silent struggling, retreat hastily. Silence. The ROMANS *all rub their noses.*

SCIPIO. [*Speaking through his nose*] Did you notice, gentlemen, that they didn't even scream? A bad omen! I prefer a screamer.

FIRST ROMAN. What's to be done now?

SECOND ROMAN. How I long for a domestic life!

THIRD ROMAN. And I for a family hearthstone. What is life without a family hearthstone? Now that Rome's founded—hang it all—I'd like a little rest.

THE FAT ROMAN. Unfortunately, gentlemen, not a single one of us understands the psychology of the other sex. Busied with wars and the founding of Rome, we have become crude, we have lost our polish, we have forgotten what a woman is——

PAULUS. [*Modestly*] Not all of us.

SCIPIO. However, from the fact that these women once had husbands—whom we routed yesterday—I draw the conclusion that there exists some means, some mysterious method, of approaching a woman whom you do not know. But how find out what it is?

THE FAT ROMAN. Suppose we ask the women themselves.

FIRST ROMAN. They won't tell.

Spiteful laughter among the WOMEN.

SECOND ROMAN. Sh! They can hear us.

SCIPIO. Well, now, I've thought of a plan——

THE FAT ROMAN. Wise head!

SCIPIO. As for our charming captives, it strikes me, gentlemen, that far from our capturing them, they have captured us. Busied in scratching our faces, tearing out our hair, and tickling us in the armpits, they obviously cannot hear us.

Not being able to hear us, they are not open to persuasion. Not being open to persuasion, they are not persuaded. So there you are!

Repeating "So there you are!" the ROMANS *fall into a state of gloomy meditation. The* WOMEN *listen attentively.*

SCIPIO. Well, here is my plan. Let us, in accordance with military custom, select an envoy from our number, and ask our fair opponents to do the same. The representatives of the warring factions, being thus in complete security [*he feels of his nose*] under the protection of the white flag, will be able, if I may employ a Latin expression, to reach a *modus vivendi*, and then——

The ROMANS *interrupt this brilliant speech with loud hurrahs.* SCIPIO, *being unanimously elected envoy, raises the white flag and cautiously approaches the* WOMEN, *at the same time calling over his shoulder:* "Don't get too far away, fellows."

SCIPIO. [*In an ingratiating tone*] Fair ladies—please stay where you are, ladies, you see I'm under the protection of the white flag, and the white flag, I assure you, is sacred, and my person is inviolable—it really is— Fair ladies! Although it was only yesterday that we had the pleasure of capturing you, already there have arisen between us disagreements, feuds, and strange misunderstandings.

CLEOPATRA. What impudence! Just because you have tied a white rag to a stick you needn't think you can make these insulting speeches.

SCIPIO. [*In a conciliatory tone*] Mercy me! Insulting speeches? Quite the contrary. I am delighted—that is to say, we are all of us perfectly miserable. [*With the courage of despair*] I swear by Hercules we are dead in love with you. Madam, since you seem to sympathise with us, I venture to ask a slight favour. Please select from your number, as we have done, an envoy——

CLEOPATRA. Oh, we know. We have already heard of it. You needn't repeat.

SCIPIO. Why, we hardly spoke above a whisper.

VOICES OF THE WOMEN. Well, we heard, just the same.

CLEOPATRA. You go back with that rag where you belong, and wait. We are going to talk this matter over. No—farther off, if you please. No eavesdropping. Who is that suckling yonder with his mouth wide open? [*Pointing at the dreaming* PAULUS] Take him away, please.

THE ROMANS. [*Whispering to one another*] Now we're getting on.

They withdraw on tiptoe, some showing their good faith by plugging their ears.

FIRST SABINE WOMAN. How impudent! How insulting! What odious tyranny! Oh, our poor husbands!

SECOND SABINE WOMAN. I swear I'll scratch out a thousand eyes before I will be disloyal for one instant to my unhappy husband. Sleep sweetly, my beloved. In the keeping of this brave heart your honour is safe.

THIRD SABINE WOMAN. I also swear.

FOURTH SABINE WOMAN. And I.

CLEOPATRA. Alas, my dear companions, we can all of us swear, but what's the use? These rude, uncultured men are no respecters of oaths. Take my captor, for instance. Although I bit his nose——

FIRST SABINE WOMAN. Oh, do you remember yours?

CLEOPATRA. [*Spitefully*] I shall remember him to my dying day. He smelled of breastplates and swords and all the other things that go with a coarse soldier. And he was so careless about squeezing me. Oh, my poor, dear husband!

First Sabine Woman. Well, they all have that soldiery smell.

Second Sabine Woman. And they all squeeze like bears. Probably it is the military fashion.

Third Sabine Woman. When I was a little girl I remember a soldier boy came to our house and said he was from a far-off country where——

Cleopatra. Ladies, this is no place for reminiscences.

Third Sabine Woman. But this soldier boy I was telling you about——

Cleopatra. My dear Juno, what in Venus's name have we to do with your soldier when every one of us has on her neck a soldier of her own? Now, my dears, what is to be done? Here is my proposition——

Veronica. [*Who has awakened, approaches. She is thin and impressively tall. Languidly, her eyes half closed, she interrupts* Cleopatra] Where are they? Why are they so far off? I wish they would come nearer. I am ashamed when they are not by me. All this time I have been in a trance, and now I cannot find the young man who carried me. He smelt like a soldier.

Cleopatra. There he stands, with his mouth wide open.

Veronica. I will go to him. I am consumed with shame.

Cleopatra. Hold her back! Why, Veronica, can it be that you have already forgotten your poor, dear husband?

Veronica. I swear I will never cease to love him. But why do we not go to our captors—or perhaps you are planning something else, my dears? For my part, I am ready for any fate. Let them come to us. Men are insufferably familiar as soon as you cease being angry with them.

Cleopatra. Well, my dears, my first suggestion is that we take an oath never to betray our dear, unhappy husbands.

ACT I THE SABINE WOMEN 167

However our captors may treat us, we shall remain firm as the Tarpeian rock. When I think how lonely my husband is, how he vainly calls me to his empty bed, "Cleopatra, where art thou, Cleopatra"; when I remember how he loved me— [*The* WOMEN *all weep*] Come, my dears, let us swear. They are waiting for us, you know.

SABINE WOMEN. We swear. We swear. Whatever they may do to us, we will not betray our husbands.

CLEOPATRA. There! My mind is at rest so far as the husbands are concerned. Sleep, beloved; sleep in peace. And now, ladies, the next thing is to choose an envoy as the Romans suggest, and let her——

FIRST SABINE WOMAN. Scratch his eyes out.

SECOND SABINE WOMAN. No, let her give the rascal a piece of her mind. They think we can do nothing but scratch; let them hear how we can talk.

VERONICA. [*Shrugging her lean shoulders*] What is the use of talking when they have us in their power?

CLEOPATRA. Stop her! Ah, Veronica, might is not right, whatever Roman law may say. Make me your envoy, and I will convince our captors that they have no right to detain us, that they are in duty bound to let us go, that according to divine law, or human law, or any other law, as they say in Rome, they have acted like perfect swine.

VOICES OF WOMEN. Go, Cleopatra; do go.

FIRST SABINE WOMAN. Stop Veronica.

CLEOPATRA. Hello, there, you envoy with the white rag! Come here, please. I want to talk with you.

SCIPIO. Shall I remove my sword?

CLEOPATRA. Never mind. Why should you? You needn't think we are afraid of your swords. Come, now, don't be frightened. I shan't bite. You weren't timid yesterday night when you broke into our peaceful home and rudely tore me from the arms of my poor husband. Well, come on, if you are coming.

> SCIPIO *approaches cautiously. The* ROMANS *and the* SABINE WOMEN *arrange themselves at right and left of the stage in two symmetrical groups and follow the parley attentively.*

SCIPIO. I am charmed, madam——

CLEOPATRA. Charmed, indeed! Let me tell you that you are a scoundrel, a lunatic, a brigand, a thief. Oh, you murderer, you miscreant, you monster, you scum! What you have done is blasphemous, disgusting, abominable, unheard of.

SCIPIO. Madam!

CLEOPATRA. You sicken me. You make my flesh creep. I can't bear the sight of you. You smell like a soldier. If your nose were not covered with scratches, I would——

SCIPIO. Pardon me. You did the scratching.

CLEOPATRA. I? Then you are the man who— [*Looks at him contemptuously*] Excuse me. I didn't recognise you.

SCIPIO. [*Joyfully*] But I recognised you instantly. Your hair smells of verbena; doesn't it, now?

CLEOPATRA. None of your business what it smells of. Verbena perfume is as good as any other.

SCIPIO. Just what I meant.

CLEOPATRA. I don't care what you meant. I've said nothing about your odours. And, anyway, why all this silly gabble about smells? I beg you, my dear sir, as a man of honour, to come to the point. What do you want of us?

> SCIPIO *modestly lowers his eyes, but, unable to hold himself in, snickers behind his hand. All the* ROMANS *snicker and the* WOMEN *bridle.*

CLEOPATRA. [*Blushing*] Snickering is no answer. You're just horrid! I ask you, what do you want of us? I suppose you know that we are already married.

SCIPIO. How shall I put it, madam? We are ready to offer you our hands and hearts——

CLEOPATRA. What! You really mean it? Are you crazy?

SCIPIO. Look at us. We are no dandies from the Nevski. Having just founded Rome, we are eager to eternalise our— Put yourself in our place, madam, and have pity on us. Would you not pity your husbands if they woke up some fine morning and found their wives missing? We are lonely, madam.

THE FAT ROMAN. Oh, so lonely.

VERONICA. [*Wiping her eyes*] I'm so sorry for them.

SCIPIO. In the midst of war's alarms, busied in the founding of Rome, we have let slip, so to speak, the moment when— Madam, we pity your husbands from the bottom of our hearts.

CLEOPATRA. [*With dignity*] I am pleased to hear you say so.

SCIPIO. But why the devil did they give you up?

The ROMANS *joyfully support him with:* "That's right"; "You've struck it, Scipio"; *but the* WOMEN *show resentment and utter such exclamations as:* "How mean of them!" "They're insulting our husbands." "The insinuating wretches!"

CLEOPATRA. [*Drily*] If you wish to go on with this parley, I beg of you to refer to our husbands with respect.

SCIPIO. With the greatest pleasure. But, madam, respect them as we may, we cannot but admit that they are unworthy of you. At this very moment, when your inhuman sufferings are pulling at our heart-strings, when the hot tears evoked by your bereavement are pouring forth like mountain brooks in spring, when the very stones, quivering with pity, moan and repine, when your charming noses, drenched with cruel tears, lose their wonted form and begin to swell——

CLEOPATRA. Nothing of the kind.

SCIPIO. When all nature, and so forth— Well, where are

your husbands now? I don't see them. They are invisible. They are absent. They have abandoned you. Shall I say, at the risk of offending, they have basely deserted you?

> *The* ROMANS *stand in a haughty pose, with arms akimbo. Excitement and tears on the part of the* WOMEN. *The gentle voice of* PROSERPINA *is heard, saying:* "Really, why are they not here? It's high time."

CLEOPATRA. All very fine, and your pose is certainly handsome, but suppose people should take it into their heads to come by night and steal us?

SCIPIO. We shall be on the alert all night long.

CLEOPATRA. Or in the daytime?

SCIPIO. Oh, you wouldn't think of going in the daytime.

> *The languid voice of* VERONICA: "Why are they so far away? I am ashamed when they are so far away. I want them to come nearer."
>
> *Whispers among the* WOMEN: "Make her keep still."

CLEOPATRA. Well, of all the impudence! Still, I am sorry for you, and I really must confess to some respect and consideration for your sufferings, though your youth has led you astray. However, I shall now advance an argument that will at one blow shatter your air-castles and, I hope, put you to blush. How about the children, sir?

SCIPIO. Wh—what children?

CLEOPATRA. The children we have left at home.

SCIPIO. That, madam, is, I confess, a serious question. Permit me to withdraw for a moment in order to confer with my companions.

> CLEOPATRA *goes to the* WOMEN, SCIPIO *to the men. They confer in whispers.*

SCIPIO. Madam.

CLEOPATRA. What is it?

SCIPIO. After protracted consideration, my companions,

ACT I THE SABINE WOMEN

the Ancient Romans, have instructed me to communicate to you that you will have new children.

CLEOPATRA. [*Staggered*] Oh, do you think so?

SCIPIO. We swear it. Gentlemen, swear!

The ROMANS *swear in a discordant chorus.*

CLEOPATRA. But the surroundings are very unattractive.

SCIPIO. [*Offended*] The surroundings?

CLEOPATRA. Yes. This is a horrid place—all mountains and ravines—simply impossible! What's this stone doing here? Take it away, please.

SCIPIO. Oh, madam! [*Carries the stone away.*

CLEOPATRA. And such trees! I'm fairly stifled here. What is this stupid tree? But you are embarrassed, aren't you? Permit me to withdraw. I suppose I must give you an answer.

SCIPIO. An answer? What to?

CLEOPATRA. Why, I thought you asked me a question.

SCIPIO. I? Pardon me, madam, I must be getting stupid. What did I ask you a question about?

CLEOPATRA. Do you mean to insult me?

SCIPIO. I?

CLEOPATRA. Yes, you. You said you were getting stupid.

SCIPIO. I?

CLEOPATRA. Certainly, *I* didn't say so. You are forgetting yourself, sir.

SCIPIO. I?

CLEOPATRA. Well, anyway, I am going. And you, sir, had better spruce up a little if we are to continue to talk to one another. You *are* a sight. Haven't you a handkerchief? Wipe your face. It is as sweaty as if you had been carrying stones all day long. [*She makes as if to withdraw.*

SCIPIO. Madam—allow me—I believe I did carry a stone or two, but the fact is you made me do it.

CLEOPATRA. I? Why, I never thought of such a thing.

SCIPIO. Begging your pardon, madam, what are we talking about?

CLEOPATRA. How should I know? That's your affair, not mine.

SCIPIO. Evidently you're making fun of me.

CLEOPATRA. Oh, you've noticed it?

SCIPIO. I won't allow myself to be ridiculed.

CLEOPATRA. How can you prevent it?

SCIPIO. I'm still a bachelor, thank God!

CLEOPATRA. Aha! At last, "thank God!" Well said, my dear sir. A nice box we should have been in if we had trusted to your oaths. [*To her companions*] Do you hear? They are already thankful that we are not their wives.

SCIPIO. Heavens! This is unendurable. Either you stop making fun of me——

CLEOPATRA. Or else——

SCIPIO. Or else go home. Yes, madam, go home. This is the limit. By Hercules, we didn't found Rome just for the sake of sticking fast, like flies in marmalade, in your absurd deliberations!

CLEOPATRA. Absurd?

SCIPIO. Yes, idiotic.

CLEOPATRA. [*Weeping*] You insult me.

SCIPIO. Good Lord! She's crying. Madam, what do you want? Why did you pick on me? Ancient Roman though I am, this woman will positively drive me crazy. Stop your crying! I can't make head or tail of this thing. I don't even know what you are blubbering about.

CLEOPATRA. [*Weeping*] Will you let us go?

SCIPIO. Certainly, certainly. Friends, Romans, do you agree? I'm at the end of my rope.

ACT I   THE SABINE WOMEN   173

FAT ROMAN. Yes, let them go. We'll fetch some wives from Etruria.

SCIPIO. All right. These creatures are not women. They are——

CLEOPATRA. [*Weeping*] On your word of honour?

SCIPIO. What am I to do on my word of honour?

CLEOPATRA. You will let us go? Perhaps your promise is just a trick, and as soon as we start to go you will lay hold of us.

SCIPIO. No, no. Run along. Are you glued to the spot?

CLEOPATRA. [*Weeping*] Will you carry us back?

SCIPIO. Heavens and earth! What next?

CLEOPATRA. You know very well that having brought us here you are in honour bound to carry us back again. It's a long way.

> The WOMEN *laugh maliciously.* SCIPIO, *panting with anger, casts frenzied glances about, but, after trying in vain to say something, stamps his foot and goes back to his friends. All the* ROMANS *pointedly turn their backs to the* WOMEN, *and sit in that position during the following scene. The* WOMEN *confer quietly.*

CLEOPATRA. You have heard, my dears; they are letting us go.

VERONICA. How dreadful!

SECOND SABINE WOMAN. You might better say, "driving us away." It's simply maddening! Here they carry off perfectly innocent women—rouse the whole house in the middle of the night—turn all the furniture upside down—wake up the children—and then, if you please—don't want us!

FIRST SABINE WOMAN. And our poor husbands! Their sufferings are in vain.

SECOND SABINE WOMAN. Just think of it—in the night-time, when everybody was asleep!

THIRD SABINE WOMAN. Say, do you know the way back?

FOURTH SABINE WOMAN. You don't suppose, do you, that I was observing the road? Of course I don't. I only know it is dreadfully far.

THIRD SABINE WOMAN. Well, it's obvious they won't carry us back.

Subdued laughter.

VERONICA. [*Moaning*] Oh, my dear boy! See, they've made him turn his back to me! I am going to him.

FIRST SABINE WOMAN. Wait a moment, Veronica. Your boy won't leave you. We must talk this thing over.

PROSERPINA. I wonder whether, after all, it is not all the same what husbands we have, whether those or these. The others were all right and these are all right. I am sure, at least, that the very first thing mine will ask of me is to make him a hot porridge. I'd rather enjoy having a new husband. The old one is sick of my menu, but this gawk will enjoy it.

CLEOPATRA. For shame, Proserpina! History will condemn us.

PROSERPINA. A lot history will understand about our doings! And here in Rome it's not so very bad, after all.

CLEOPATRA. You're horrid, Proserpina. Just suppose they should be listening to us! But here's my plan, my dears. Though we are, of course, going home at once to our dear, late husbands, it is a long walk, and we are tired.

FIRST SABINE WOMAN. My nerves are completely shattered!

SECOND SABINE WOMAN. No constitution could stand it! All of a sudden in the middle of the night to wake up the whole house——

CLEOPATRA. So let's stay here a day or two and rest. That will please them and commit us to nothing. Besides, when they see how cheerful and modest we are, our captors will find it easier to part with us. I confess, too, that I am a little sorry for mine. His nose is a sight.

THIRD SABINE WOMAN. But we'll stay only two days!

FOURTH SABINE WOMAN. One day will be enough for me. We'll just take a little walk— Hurry, Cleopatra, I think they have already fallen asleep.

CLEOPATRA. [*To* SCIPIO] Sir!

SCIPIO. [*Not turning around*] What you want?

CLEOPATRA. Come here a moment, please.

SCIPIO. At your service, madam.

CLEOPATRA. We have decided to accept your kind offer and to go away at once. You are not angry?

SCIPIO. Not at all.

CLEOPATRA. But first we should like to rest a little. Will you let us stay here a day or so and rest? This is a lovely spot.

All the ROMANS *simultaneously turn around and spring to their feet.*

SCIPIO. [*In ecstasy*] Dear madam! What has the place to do with it, and what—? O Jupiter! Madam, I swear by Hercules, I swear by Venus, I swear by Bacchus! Madam, may I be thrice anathema if— I swear by Aphrodite! Gentlemen, Ancient Romans! Board the ship!

CLEOPATRA. I suggest that we take a little stroll.

SCIPIO. Oh, madam! Gentlemen, Romans! Foot-pace! Dress front! left, right; left, right! Column of twos! [*He seizes* CLEOPATRA *by the arm and leads her toward the hills. At his command the* ROMANS, *each seizing a* SABINE WOMAN, *proudly march in file behind him.*] Left, right; left, right! One, two; one, two!

PAULUS EMILIUS. [*Left dreaming alone upon the stage, rushes about, crying pitifully*] Where is she? Gentlemen, Ancient Romans, wait! I have lost her. Where is she?

VERONICA *stands like a bride, her eyes modestly cast down.*

PAULUS. [*Flying toward her blindly*] Beg your pardon, madam, have you seen her?

VERONICA. You stupid!

PAULUS. I?

VERONICA. Yes, stupid!

PAULUS. Why, what are you scolding me for?

VERONICA. Scolding you! You silly! Can't you see? Oh, my darling boy! I have waited for you thirty years! Oh, take——

PAULUS. Take what?

VERONICA. Me. You see it is I, she— Oh, you stupid thing!

PAULUS. You? No, you are not the right one.

VERONICA. Yes, I am.

PAULUS. No, you're not. [*He sits on the ground and weeps.*

VERONICA. See, they have left us alone, and I am ashamed. Come!

PAULUS. [*Weeps*] You are not the right one.

VERONICA. But I say I am, plague take you! Did any one ever see the like! My husband repeated that phrase, "You are the wrong one," for thirty years, and now this suckling is at it. Give me your hand.

PAULUS. [*Gets up in terror*] You are the wrong one. Oh, oh, oh, save me! She has captured me!

Curtain.

ACT II

A scene shrouded in gloom, symbolising the sad plight of the bereaved husbands. Possibly rain is falling, and the wind whistling, and perhaps black clouds cover the sky; but very likely it just seems so. At any rate, the gloom is horrible.[1]
As the curtain rises the disposition of the characters is as follows: At the sides, in two symmetrical groups, a part of the SABINE MEN *are engaged in gymnastic exercises. As they move their arms they repeat with rapt attention:* "Twenty-five minutes' daily drill will banish every pain and ill." *In the middle of the stage, on a long bench, sit in a row the husbands who have children. Each one holds a baby in his arms. Their heads droop wearily to one side and their attitudes dramatise despair. It is a distressing picture. For a long time nothing is heard but the ominous, barely audible whisper:* "Twenty-five minutes' daily drill——"

Enter ANCUS MARTIUS, *exhibiting from a distance a letter.*

MARTIUS. The address, Sabines! The address of our wives! The address, gentlemen, the address!

HUSHED VOICES. Hear! Hear! The address! The address! We have the address!

ANCUS MARTIUS *quickly takes from his pocket a little bell and jingles it.*

VOICES. Silence! Silence!

---

[1] The *mise en scène* should suggest that the husbands are plunged in grief and would like to be relieved of it.

MARTIUS. Gentlemen, Sabines, history will not reproach us either for dilatoriness or indecision. Neither dilatoriness nor indecision are traits of the Sabine, whose stormy, impetuous character can scarcely be restrained by the floodgates of reason and experience. Recall, plundered husbands, whither we rushed on the memorable morning which followed the memorable night when those brigands basely kidnapped our hapless wives. Do you recall, Sabines, whither our nimble legs carried us, devouring space, annihilating all obstacles, and filling the land with din. Come, recall, gentlemen!

The SABINES *maintain a timid silence.*

MARTIUS. Come, come, recall, gentlemen!

A TIMID VOICE. Proserpina, Proserpina, my darling! Where art thou? O-o-o-oh!

The SABINES, *in rapt silence, gaze at the mouth of the speaker.*

ANCUS MARTIUS. [*Without waiting for an answer, cries impressively*] To the Information Bureau! That's where. But recall, gentlemen, our grief. That effete institution as yet knew nothing and gave us no correction of their previous addresses. And, having for a whole week replied to our inquiries with ever the same cruel irony, it finally responded in these burning words [*he reads*]: "Left for parts unknown." But, Sabines, did we rest satisfied? Recall.

SABINES *maintain silence.*

MARTIUS. No, we did not rest satisfied. Here is a dry but eloquent enumeration of our achievements in these brief eighteen months. We have inserted advertisements in all reputable newspapers, with promises of reward to the finder. We have summoned all the prominent astrologers, and every night from their observation of the stars they have sought to divine the address of our hapless wives——

ACT II THE SABINE WOMEN

A TIMID VOICE. Proserpina, my darling, o-o-o-oh!

MARTIUS. Not only have we sacrificed one thousand chickens, geese, and ducks, but we have disembowelled all the cats in our endeavours by the inspection of birds and animals to determine the portentous address. But, alas, through the will of the gods our superhuman efforts have been frustrated! Recall, Sabines— However, it's not necessary. I will only add that neither experimental nor theoretical science has given us an answer. Even the constellations, to which our gaze was turned with sorrowful inquiry, though they deigned to reply, were no more definite than the Information Bureau: Left, left, left! Whither? For parts unknown!

Subdued weeping among the SABINES.

A TIMID VOICE. Proserpina! Oh! Proserpina!

MARTIUS. Yes, Sabines, a strange answer to receive from the constellations when one considers that from their point of vantage the whole universe is visible. But I continue with pride the enumeration of our achievements. Recall, gentlemen, what our learned jurists were doing while the astrologers were conjecturing from the stars. Come, now, recall!

The SABINES *maintain silence.*

MARTIUS. Come, recall, gentlemen. It's strenuous work talking to you. You stand like statues; by Heaven, you do! I am sure you remember, only you are modest about speaking. Come, now, gentlemen; come, come, come, recall! What were our jurists doing while——

A TIMID VOICE. Proserpina, o-o-o-oh! o-o-o-oh!

MARTIUS. Silence, there! Why are you eternally dragging in your Proserpina? Well, I will help you, gentlemen. Do you remember why we are practising gymnastics? Come, come!

A TIMID VOICE. [*From the back row*] To develop our muscles.

MARTIUS. To be sure, and very well said. And now, why do we need muscles? Come, come, answer up! Gentlemen, you wear one's patience completely out. Jog your memories. Why do we need muscles, Sabines?

A HESITATING VOICE. To fight with.

MARTIUS. [*Raising his arms to heaven in despair*] Ye Heavens! "To fight with!" And I hear that from a Sabine, a friend of the law, a patron of order, the only genuine example of a legal conscience in the world! "To fight with!" I am ashamed of this ruffianly breach of etiquette appropriate only to the brigand Romans, the base kidnappers of our absolutely legal wives.

A TIMID VOICE. Oh, Proserpina, Proserpina!

MARTIUS. Hold your tongue, will you? Proserpina, indeed! Just when we are getting down to general principles you must come in with your maundering about Proserpina! But I see, gentlemen, that this bereavement has somewhat dimmed your usually brilliant memories, and so I repeat in brief: We need muscles in order that, having learned the address and entered upon our march against the Romans —do you understand?—we may be able to carry the entire distance the heavy code of laws, the collection of enactments and decisions on appeal, and also—do you understand now?—the four hundred volumes of investigations which our jurists have compiled on the question of the legality of our marriages—eh, do you understand?—and on the illegality of kidnapping. Our weapons, Sabines, are the justice of our cause and a clear conscience. We will prove to the base kidnappers that they *are* kidnappers, and to our wives we will prove that they were kidnapped, and Heaven will shudder; for now that the address is found, it's all up with the Romans. Look! [*He shakes the letter and the* SABINES, *standing on tiptoe, peek at it*] Here is a registered letter signed "A

Repentant Kidnapper." In it some unknown friend expresses repentance for his thoughtless crime. He assures us that he will no longer kidnap, and prays that fate may have mercy upon him. The name is undecipherable—blurred by a big blot where, apparently, tears have fallen. There, gentlemen! That is the power of conscience! He also informs us, by the way, that the hearts of our wives are broken——

A TIMID VOICE. Proserpin——

MARTIUS. Please listen, will you? Between you and your Proserpina I cannot get a word in edgewise. Proserpina, you must remember, is a mere detail, and yet at a time when we are all with such enthusiasm working out general problems, when we are formulating a plan—I'll tell you about it presently—when we are preparing for victory or death, you whine for some insignificant Proserpina or somebody. In the name of the assembly, I call you to order. And now, gentlemen, forward! Attention! Form in rank and file! Come, step lively, gentlemen! Oh, this is maddening! You cannot even yet distinguish right from left. Where are you going? Where are you going? Halt! [*He seizes a* SABINE *who is out of line and instructs him*] In order to learn which your right foot is, you must stand still and look at me. Now place yourself with your face to the north—or, no, with your face to the south and your back to the east. Now, where is your face? Man, that is not your face, that is your back. See, here is your face; can't you understand? Oh, this is intolerable! If you want to know which your right foot is, look at your neighbour. Now, gentlemen, which of you have penknives? Turn your pockets inside out. Good. Toothpicks? Leave them behind. Not a suggestion of violence, gentlemen; nothing that pricks or cuts. Our weapons are a clear conscience and the justice of our cause. Now each one of you take up a volume of the laws and investigations. Good! They ought to be bound, but we'll attend to that later. Now you see what muscles are for! Very good, very good. Trumpeters to the front! Remember, you're to play "The March of the Plundered Husbands." Forw— Hold on! Do you remember how to march?

The SABINES *remain silent.*

MARTIUS. You don't? Well, I will remind you. Two steps forward, one step backward; two steps forward, one step backward. The first two steps are designed to indicate, Sabines, the unquenchable fire of our stormy souls, the firm will, the irresistible advance. The step backward symbolises the step of reason, the step of experience and of the mature mind. In taking that step we ponder the outcome of our acts. In taking it we also maintain, as it were, a close bond with tradition, with our ancestors, with our great past. History makes no leaps, and we, Sabines, at this great moment, we are history. Trumpeters, trumpet!

> *The trumpets emit a doleful wail, which, now convulsively lurching forward and now smoothly and gently swaying backward, carries with it the whole army of plundered husbands. Taking two steps forward and one step backward, they slowly pass across the stage.*[1]
>
> *The curtain falls. The trumpets blare wearily and the second scene passes into the third.*

[1] The St. Petersburg theatre, "The Convex Mirror," very successfully adapted for this scene the air of the "Marseillaise." In the first two measures the trumpets sounded boldly and triumphantly, while in the succeeding measure they emitted a kind of belch as mournful as it was distressing.

ACT III

The same wild scene as in the first act, though there are now some traces of orderliness. Near one of the huts stands a ROMAN *in a lazy attitude, blissfully picking his nose. In the background, at the left, the army of husbands is seen marching with concentrated attention in the same manner as before: two steps forward, one step backward. The* ROMAN, *on catching sight of them, shows at first signs of animation, and, ceasing to attend to his nose, watches them with good-natured curiosity. The slowness of their movements, however, apparently makes him drowsy. He yawns, stretches languidly, and seats himself leisurely on a stone. At a signal from* ANCUS MARTIUS *the trumpets cease.*

MARTIUS. [*In a tone of despair*] Halt, Sabines! Halt, will you?

The SABINES *halt as if rooted to the spot.*

MARTIUS. Come, halt, will you? Oh, Heavens! Will nothing hold back this falling avalanche? Will nothing— Thank God, they have halted! Attention! Trumpeters, to the rear! Professors, to the front. The rest, attention!

The TRUMPETERS *withdraw, the* PROFESSORS *advance. The rest stand as if fettered.*

MARTIUS. Professors, make ready!

The PROFESSORS *quickly squat down, unfold little tables, lay upon each table a thick book, and open the covers with a clatter. The effect is something like the firing of a field-battery. The* ROMAN (*it is* SCIPIO), *waking up, apparently becomes interested and inquires in a friendly manner:* "What is the matter, gentlemen? What can I do for you? If this is a circus, I take the liberty to inform you that the Colosseum is not yet finished."

MARTIUS. [*Calmly*] Silence, base kidnapper! [*To the* SABINES] And now, Sabines, we have reached the wished-for goal. Behind us is the long path of privation, hunger, solitude, and canned fruit. Before us a struggle such as history has never known. Be inspired, Sabines, but control yourselves; be tranquil. Maintaining a spirit of natural indignation, calmly await the fated end. Recall, Sabines, why we have come here.

The SABINES *are silent.*

MARTIUS. Come, recall, gentlemen! We surely did not come here with these huge books merely to take a walk! Come, recall, gentlemen. Why are we here?

SCIPIO. Come, come, gentlemen, recall.

MARTIUS. [*To* SCIPIO] Just think of it, they're always like that!

SCIPIO. You don't mean it!

MARTIUS. It's a fact. They stand like graven images. They can do nothing but blink their eyes. Tell me, now—Can one deliver a first-class speech without resorting to the exclamation "Recall, gentlemen"?

SCIPIO. [*Good-naturedly shaking his head*] Well, scarcely. It would be a queer speech.

MARTIUS. There! Of course it would. Even you understand that, but as for these fellows——

From the ranks of the SABINES *comes a tremulous voice:*
"Oh, Proserpina, my darling, where art thou? O-o-o-oh!"

SCIPIO. [*Puzzled*] He must be recalling.

MARTIUS. [*Contemptuously*] Oh, he is always recalling.

ACT III THE SABINE WOMEN 185

[*To the* SABINES] Attention! We are now going to make a peremptory demand for our wives. Woe to the abductors if their conscience has not yet awakened! We will have the law of them. Oh, base abductor; summon your base companions and prepare for the dire penalty!

SCIPIO. I will call my wife at once.

> *He goes into the hut, calling:* "Cleopatra! Come out, please; some one wants to see you on business!"
>
> PAULUS EMILIUS *peeks from around the corner and, recognising the* SABINES, *shouts joyfully:* "The husbands have come! The husbands have come! Ancient Romans, wake up! The husbands are here!"
>
> *He rushes to* MARTIUS *and, with tears in his eyes, hangs upon his neck.* MARTIUS *is nonplussed.* PAULUS *hurries on, repeating the joyous cry:* "The husbands are here!"
>
> *The drowsy* ROMANS *crawl out of their huts and take up a position on the right side of the stage.* MARTIUS, *in a dramatic pose, haughtily waits until they are assembled.*

THE FAT ROMAN. By Bacchus! I have had as delightful a sleep as on the day we founded Rome. What's that row of dummies?

FIRST ROMAN. Sh! That's the husbands.

THE FAT ROMAN. Heavens, but I'm thirsty! Proserpina, my pet, bring me some cider!

> *From the ranks of the* SABINES *comes a faint cry:* "Proserpina! O-o-o-oh!"

THE FAT ROMAN. What does he want? Is he, too, calling my wife?

FIRST ROMAN. Sh! That's her husband.

THE FAT ROMAN. Oh, I forgot! Heavens, but I am thirsty! After that hot porridge and a sound sleep I could drink a lake dry. And what porridge Proserpina can make! Really, Romans, it is a gift of the gods!

FIRST ROMAN. Sh!

THE FAT ROMAN. The deuce, I forgot! But I had the queerest dream just now. I thought I was asleep and suddenly I saw Rome beginning to fall, fall, fall—and then it fell.

FIRST ROMAN. But how about our wives? Although they have callers, they do not appear. It's an awkward situation.

SECOND ROMAN. Probably they are dressing.

FIRST ROMAN. Oh, woman, thy name is vanity! One might expect them to say, "Pooh! it's only my late husband!" but no, they can't escape the eternal feminine. Really, the psychology of woman is beyond me!

THE FAT ROMAN. Heavens, but I am thirsty! How long are those Egyptian mummies going to stand there? They have trumpets. They might at least strike up a tune. Look! Look! They move!

MARTIUS. Romans, at last we stand face to face. I trust that, setting aside all dissimulation, you will give us a direct and honest answer. Do you recall, Romans, the deed you committed on the night between the 20th and the 21st of April?

The ROMANS *look at one another in embarrassed silence.*

MARTIUS. Come, recall! Is it possible you cannot recall? Try to recall, gentlemen. I assure you, I shall not stir a step until you recall.

THE FAT ROMAN. [*Terrified, whispers to another*] Maybe you can remember, Agrippa? It must have been something important, huh?

Remarks by the ROMANS: "No, I can't remember anything." "I must have lost my memory while I was asleep." "I'd better go; you can tell me about it afterward." "Really, what does he want?"

MARTIUS. [*In a loud voice*] Then I will remind you, Romans. On the night between the 20th and 21st of April there was committed the greatest crime known to history. Certain individuals—I will disclose their identity later—villainously abducted our wives, the beautiful Sabine women.

> *The* ROMANS, *remembering, confirm the statement with joyful noddings of the head:* "Yes, yes, yes, yes!" "Ho! That's what is on foot!" "Perfectly true. 'Twas the 20th of April."

THE FAT ROMAN. [*Deeply impressed*] These Sabines have heads!

MARTIUS. And you were the abductors, Romans! Oh, I know you will attempt to justify yourselves. You will distort the facts. You will basely pervert the legal norms, taking refuge in that abominable casuistry which is inevitably linked with every violation of right. But we are prepared. Professors, begin!

> *The* PROFESSOR *at the end of the line begins speaking in a monotonous voice that seems to come from beyond the bounds of space and time:* "Concerning Crimes against Property; volume one, division one, chapter one, page one, entitled On the Subject of Robbery in General. In very ancient times, far more ancient than the present time, when birds, insects, and beetles fearlessly hopped about in the sunlight and no violations of justice entered into their consciousness, inasmuch as there was no consciousness—in those remote times——"

MARTIUS. Attention, Romans, attention!

SCIPIO. Can't you make it shorter?

MARTIUS. Can't be done.

SCIPIO. But your hearers will go to sleep.

MARTIUS. Do you think so?

SCIPIO. Why, as you see, they are already dozing, and when they are dozing they don't hear anything. Can't you begin at the other end, eh? Come, be so good as to say straight out what you want.

MARTIUS. In sooth, this is a strange argument! But be it so. Condescending to the weakness of your friends, I will tell you directly that we want to prove to you that you were wrong when you abducted our wives, and that you Romans are abductors, and that by no subtleties of sophistry will you succeed in justifying your base act! Even the heavens will shudder!

SCIPIO. Really, really, my dear fellow, we don't even deny it.

MARTIUS. You don't? Then why have we come here?

SCIPIO. I don't know. Perhaps you were out for a stroll.

MARTIUS. No, we came on purpose to prove these things to you. It's very odd. Then you agree that you are abductors?

SCIPIO. Unreservedly. And I find the word "abductors" very appropriate.

MARTIUS. But perhaps you are not thoroughly convinced of it? In that case the professor is quite ready— Aren't you, Professor? Are you not quite ready to——

SCIPIO. Oh, no! You mustn't. We are thoroughly convinced. Romans, back me up or he will begin again!

ROMANS. Agreed, agreed!

MARTIUS. Well, then, what's all this about?

SCIPIO. I don't know.

MARTIUS. Here is a strange misunderstanding. Sabines,

celebrate your triumph! They confess their guilt. The mere appearance of our threatening preparations has awakened in them the powerful voice of legal conscience, and Heaven itself has shuddered. It only remains for us, in the consciousness of having performed our duty, to return and——

A TREMBLING VOICE. But my Proserpina?

MARTIUS. Ah, yes! Inappropriate though your expression may be, you have the right idea—quite right, my friend. Romans, here is a complete and accurate list of the names of our wives. Be so kind as to return them to us. For all loss, all damage—what's the wording of your law there, Professor?

PROFESSOR. Tare and tret.

MARTIUS. No, no! "Injury!" Yes, for every injury you will be held responsible. Read the entire section, Professor. However—here are our wives. Attention, Sabines! Maintain your self-control, I beseech you. Restrain the outburst of passion until the question of justice is settled— Two steps forward, one step backward! Halt! Greetings to you, Sabine wives! Welcome, Cleopatra!

The WOMEN *with eyes downcast and modest aspect, dignified and yet submissive, occupy the centre of the stage.*

CLEOPATRA. [*Without raising her eyes*] If you have come to scold, Ancus Martius, let me tell you that we do not deserve your reproaches. We struggled long and did not yield except on compulsion. I swear to you, beloved Martius, I have not for a single moment ceased to weep for you.

She weeps and, taking her cue, all the SABINE WOMEN *weep.*

MARTIUS. Calm yourself, Cleopatra. They have already confessed that they are abductors. Let us now return to our household gods, Cleopatra.

CLEOPATRA. [*Without raising her eyes*] I fear that you will scold us, but we have become accustomed to this location. Don't you like these hills, Martius?

MARTIUS. I don't understand you, Cleopatra. What have the hills to do with it?

CLEOPATRA. I fear you will be angry, but, really, we are not to blame. I have already wept for you in due form, Martius, and now I cannot understand at all what you want. More tears? Oh, as many as you like. My dear friends, they think we have not wept enough for them. Let us show them their error. Oh, weep, weep, my dear friends! I loved you so, Martius!

The WOMEN *shed rivers of tears.*

SCIPIO. Calm yourself, Cleopatra. Excitement is bad for you now. And you, sir, do you hear? Go back home. Come, Cleopatra, lie down and rest. I will look after the soup myself.

MARTIUS. And what has the soup to do with it, I should like to know? Calm yourself, Cleopatra, there is some misunderstanding here. Apparently you do not understand that you are abducted.

CLEOPATRA. [*Weeping*] There, I told you you were going to scold! Scipio, deary, have you my handkerchief?

SCIPIO. Here it is, precious.

MARTIUS. But I should like to know what the handkerchief has to do with it.

CLEOPATRA. [*Weeping*] What a fuss to make about a handkerchief! I cannot get on without a handkerchief when I am crying, and it is all your fault. You are a cruel monster, Ancus Martius!

> *They all weep,* SABINE WOMEN, SABINE MEN, *and even several of the* ROMANS.

THE VOICE. Proserpina! O-o-o-oh!

MARTIUS. [*In a sonorous voice*] Calm yourselves, Sabines.

Control yourselves. Don't move; I'll settle everything in a jiffy. There apparently is some misunderstanding of a legal nature. This unhappy woman thinks she is accused of stealing a handkerchief and does not even dream that she herself is stolen. We will prove this to her. Professors, begin.

The PROFESSORS *make preparations. The* ROMANS *are horror-stricken.* SCIPIO *seizes* CLEOPATRA *by the hand.*

SCIPIO. Own up, Cleopatra! Come, be quick! Heavens, he will begin in a moment!

CLEOPATRA. I have nothing to confess. It is all slander.

MARTIUS. Professor, we are waiting.

SCIPIO. Come, hurry, own up! Oh, Heavens, he is already opening his mouth! He will have it open in a minute! Sabines! Wait! She has confessed! Shut your mouth, Professor, she has confessed!

CLEOPATRA. Very well, I confess. [*To the* WOMEN] My dear friends, do you confess, too?

SCIPIO. [*Hastily*] Yes, they all confess. Everything is all right.

MARTIUS. [*In perplexity*] One moment, sir, if you please. Cleopatra, do you admit that you and the other Sabine women were abducted on the night between the 20th and the 21st of April? Do you?

CLEOPATRA. [*Spitefully*] No, we ran away of ourselves.

MARTIUS. There, you see! She doesn't understand. Mr. Profes——

CLEOPATRA. That's mean of you, Martius. You overslept. You did not defend us; you gave us up; you forgot us; you abandoned us; and now you accuse us of running away. We were abducted, Martius, basely abducted. You can read about it in any Roman history, to say nothing [*weeping*] of the encyclopedia.

SCIPIO. [*Shouting*] Come, shut your mouth, Professor!

But the PROFESSOR'S *mouth remains open. The* ROMANS *are thrown into a panic, and some rush off the stage.*

MARTIUS. Romans, Sabines, attention! I will remove the difficulty in a moment. There is some misunderstanding of a mechanical nature. Allow me to inspect you, Professor. Why, to be sure. I might have known it. The hinge is broken and he cannot shut his mouth. No matter. We will fix it up when we get home. For the present it is enough that they admit they were abducted. I have heard it with my own ears. Our goal is attained, and Heaven itself has shuddered. Let us go back to our household gods, Cleopatra.

CLEOPATRA. I don't want to go back to our household gods.

THE SABINE WOMEN. Rubbish about your household gods! We don't want to go back to our household gods. We are going to stay here. They are insulting us! They are getting ready to abduct us! Save us, help, defend us!

The ROMANS *with clattering weapons take a position between the* WOMEN *and the* SABINES *and gradually crowd the* WOMEN *into the background. They cast angry glances at the* SABINES.

VOICES. To arms, Romans! To the defence of your wives! To arms, Romans!

MARTIUS. [*Ringing his bell*] What is the matter? There will be a fight here in a minute. My brain is in a whirl. Sabines, my brain is in a whirl.

PROSERPINA. [*Coming forward and speaking in a slow, calm voice*] Don't get excited, Romans, I will speak with Martius alone.

From the ranks of the SABINES *comes a quavering voice, a mournful call of love:* "Proserpina, my darling, o-o-o-o-oh!"

PROSERPINA. [*Coolly*] Ah, my dove! How are you? Come here, Ancus Martius, and don't be afraid; your army won't run away. Do you understand that neither your wife, Cleopatra, nor we other Sabine women wish to go home? Do you understand that?

MARTIUS. I am dazed. How can I live without Cleopatra? I cannot live without Cleopatra! She is my perfectly legal wife. Do you think she won't come back on any terms?

PROSERPINA. Not on any terms.

MARTIUS. What am I to do? You see that I love her. How can I live without her? [*He weeps*.

PROSERPINA. Cheer up, Martius. [*She whispers*] I am sorry for you, and I will tell you as a secret that there is only one means, one solitary means left—abduct her!

MARTIUS. But will she come?

PROSERPINA. [*Shrugging her shoulders*] How can she help coming if you abduct her?

MARTIUS. But that would be wicked. You are suggesting to me that I commit violence. What would then become of my legal conscience, or can it be that you women believe that might is right? Oh, woman, woman!

PROSERPINA. Oh, we have heard "Woman, woman!" before. It was a leaden day when the gods made you, Martius. You are unutterably stupid. If I am to remain faithful, I want a strong man, the strongest man there is. Do you think we are so fond of being abducted and stolen, and asked back and returned, and lost and found, and——

THE VOICE. Proserpina, my darling, o-o-o-oh!

PROSERPINA. Yes, my dear. How are you—? And to have people deal with us as if we were things. I no sooner get accustomed to one man than along comes another and carries me away, and I no sooner get accustomed to the new man than the old one appears and says: "Come back." Really,

Martius, if, as you protest, you want your wife to be your own, then all you have to do is to be the strongest. Give in to no one, struggle for her tooth and nail. In short, die in her defence. Believe me, Martius, there is no greater joy for a woman than to die upon the grave of a husband who has fallen in her defence. And be assured, Martius, that a woman proves false only after her husband has proved false.

MARTIUS. But they have swords and we are weaponless.

PROSERPINA. Get swords!

MARTIUS. But they have strong muscles and we have not.

PROSERPINA. Get strong! Oh, Martius, you are an impenetrable fool!

MARTIUS. [*Springing away from her*] And you are a trifling and silly woman. Long live the law! Let them take my wife from me by brute violence; let them ruin my home; let them extinguish my hearth; I shall never prove false to the law. Let the whole world laugh at the unfortunate Sabines, they will not prove false to the law. Virtue commands respect, even in rags. Sabines, retreat! Weep, Sabines, weep bitter tears! Sob, beat your breasts, and be not ashamed of tears. Let them stone us, let them mock us, but weep! Let them besmear us with mud! Weep, Sabines; you are weeping for the scorned and down-trampled law. Forward, Sabines. Attention! Trumpeters, strike up the march. Two steps forward, one step backward; two steps forward, one step backward.

The WOMEN *begin to weep.*

CLEOPATRA. Martius, wait!

MARTIUS. Avaunt, woman, I know thee not! Slow march!

The trumpets set up a mournful wail. The WOMEN, *weeping and wailing loudly, are drawn toward their former husbands, but the* ROMANS *hold them back by force.*

Laughter on the part of the victors. Paying no attention either to the tears or the laughter, but bending under the weight of the laws, the SABINES *slowly withdraw; two steps forward, one step backward.*